T0291215

Monitoring the State or the Market

Many economists argue that economic analysis should avoid distributional consequences of policies. In democratic countries, however, the political power of individuals inevitably reflects their wealth and income. You cannot have a democracy when income and wealth distributions are greatly uneven. *Monitoring the State or the Market* explains that absolute income equality is not consistent with a market economy, yet neither is large inequality. This study provides a broad survey of major social and economic developments over the past two centuries, beginning with the Industrial Revolution and laissez faire and ending with neoliberalism and market fundamentalism. It explains how each of these periods initially brought moderation and accompanying benefits, demonstrating that some countries, like those in Scandinavia, have demonstrated that it is possible to have low Gini coefficients (low inequality), while preserving economic freedom and prosperity.

Vito Tanzi is Honorary President of the International Institute of Public Finance (IIPF). He was the Undersecretary for Economy and Finance for the Italian Government and the Director of the Fiscal Affairs Department at the International Monetary Fund. He is the recipient of five honorary degrees and has authored twenty-five books and hundreds of articles. An economic effect, the "Tanzi Effect," carries his name.

Monitoring the State or the Market

From Laissez Faire to Market Fundamentalism

VITO TANZI

International Institute of Public Finance

CAMBRIDGE
UNIVERSITY PRESS

Shaftesbury Road, Cambridge CB2 8EA, United Kingdom

One Liberty Plaza, 20th Floor, New York, NY 10006, USA

477 Williamstown Road, Port Melbourne, VIC 3207, Australia

314–321, 3rd Floor, Plot 3, Splendor Forum, Jasola District Centre,
New Delhi – 110025, India

103 Penang Road, #05-06/07, Visioncrest Commercial, Singapore 238467

Cambridge University Press is part of Cambridge University Press & Assessment,
a department of the University of Cambridge.

We share the University's mission to contribute to society through the pursuit of
education, learning and research at the highest international levels of excellence.

www.cambridge.org
Information on this title: www.cambridge.org/9781009434447

DOI: 10.1017/9781009434430

First published 2024

A catalogue record for this publication is available from the British Library

Library of Congress Cataloging-in-Publication Data

ISBN 978-1-009-43444-7 Hardback
ISBN 978-1-009-43447-8 Paperback

Contents

Preface

This book is largely the result of frustration. The frustration of someone who, for six decades, had been at the center of economic activities and economic thinking and debates, both as an academic, as a high-level supervisor of large groups of highly trained economists, in an important international organization (The International Monetary Fund), and as part of a G7 government (the Italian government). I had also been an active member of a relevant global, academic economic organization, The International Institute of Public Finance (IIPF), of which I had been President in 1990–1994 and am now Honorary President.

When I studied economics, first at the George Washington University in the 1950s. and later at Harvard in the 1960s, I had the good luck of studying under some of the leading economists of the time, several of whom would win the earliest Nobel Prizes in Economics. I learned that the field that I had chosen had the goal of promoting the economic wellbeing of communities and countries. I learned that more economic output (more economic production), when distributed fairly, though not equally, would lead to more general welfare and to happier communities. I also learned that an efficient economy, one in which individuals were guided by basic incentives, would promote self-interest, empathy for others, and community goals.

I had been aware, then, that there were some economists, called conservative, libertarian, or laissez faire economists, who, possibly influenced by the past behaviors of bad and nondemocratic governments, of which there had been many in history, or by the current behavior of socialist governments (such as those that existed in Russia and other "Soviet economies"), believed that government intervention was always bad, and was always accompanied by the danger of becoming a road to serfdom or to inefficiency, as Hayek had stressed in an influential book in the early 1940s, and as von Mises and others have continued to believe.

In the early 1960s these libertarian economists were relatively few, and their influence in the decades after the Great Depression had been limited. Their number and influence would increase in the 1970s, at a time when the economies of advanced countries were running into serious difficulties (inflation and recessions at the same time), while the centrally planned economies of the Soviet Union had also started to run into even greater trouble.

The importance of the libertarian economists, economists who believed in the miraculous work of a free market, one in which economic agents would be free from government guidance and controls, would pay low taxes and would follow the guidelines set by the free markets and by their personal incentives, grew in the late 1970s. These economists had great faith that free economic agents would respect the liberty of others, even in the absence of governments, authorities, and rules that required them to do so, and that they would not abuse the market or the natural environment.

In this free society, speed limits for cars might not be necessary, and neither would regulations that instructed individuals not to pollute or cheat others or that punished them for not respecting established rules. Individual freedom would reign supreme in this free market environment, and prosperity for the whole of society would automatically follow from the greater activity and from "trickle down." Who would not want to live in such a world?

Somehow, I always felt that the libertarian economists who were advocating economic freedom and a world largely free of taxes and regulations, (and, by implication, without essential public goods, because there would be no or little tax to finance them), were living in a dreamland. The world that they imagined possible was obviously very different from the world that had been created in the Soviet Union. But it was also very different from the world of reality as I saw it, and as even Adam Smith had seen it three centuries ago when he warned about "cartels" and other abuses of the market.

I was convinced that a world that combined the essential function of a market with a democratic government that closely monitored the market for abuses and inefficiency and paid some attention to equity was a possible, realistic, and preferable world. At least in principle, this was the world that the welfare states had been trying to create after the Second World War.

The question of whether the thinking of the libertarian economists or that of those who were creating the welfare states was right bothered me for decades. This book is an attempt to deal with that question in a way that is as objective as possible when one deals with difficult ideological questions. I hope that this book will not be seen as too one-sided, and that it can contribute to an informed debate, one that is badly needed at this time. I have no illusion that all those who read this book will be convinced by its arguments. But some may, and that would be progress.

The book is divided into three historically based sections, to distinguish different pressures that existed in those periods. Each of those periods have different characteristics and respond to different challenges and circumstances.

Acknowledgments

Several individuals were kind enough to give me some reactions and comments on earlier drafts of this book. They included: Giorgio Brosio, Nuri Erbas, George Iden, Hans-Werner Sinn, and Andres Solimano. Frequent conversions with my son, Alex Tanzi, an economic reporter with Bloomberg Net, were also useful in making me think about some current issues.

As always, I am grateful to my wife, Maria, for her continuing support and encouragement, and for providing me with the gift of the free time that was necessary for this project.

PART I

THE PERIOD UNTIL THE GREAT DEPRESSION

I

Introduction

Much of modern economic theory deals with the short-term and, because of that, it has largely cut its connection with history. Economic history is no longer a required field in many PhD economics programs. In recent decades, economic theorizing has become increasingly technical, in an attempt to make economics more and more like physics, and less and less like sociology or psychology. Economics has become much more connected with current developments, and model building has become the norm (see Solow, 2005). This was not the case a century ago when economists such as Karl Marx, Alois Schumpeter, and Edwin Seligman, who was an important professor at Colombia University, among others, had theorized about the existence of relationships between economic and historical developments (see Marx, 1867; Seligman, 1907; Schumpeter, 1942). They had theorized that, in the long-term, economic developments often lead to important social reactions.

This change in emphasis in economic analysis has had some good and some less-good consequences. While the modern approach has many advantages and has made economics look more rigorous and more scientific, making economic relations and economic articles resemble those in physics, it has failed to recognize the ways in which economics continues to be significantly different from physics. For example, economic variables are rarely precisely measured, and, at times, there are long and undefined lags between the time when a policy is enacted or some actions are taken by individuals or by the government and when their effects are fully felt in the economy. It also fails to recognize that the short-term effects of some policies may be different from those in the long-term, as had been theorized by historical determinism in the past.

The difficulties in measuring variables and the lags are often ignored by economists in their more technical, modern approach. This means that modern economics, to some extent, has become increasingly detached from historical developments and also, at times, from a longer run reality. Some psychologists, such as Kahneman, Tversky, and others, have also concluded that individuals often suffer from irrationality, so that the fundamental assumption of rational behavior on the part of market participants can lead to unexpected results.

The modern approach also tends to ignore the existence of relationships that do not lend themselves to easy, quantitative, or econometric estimations but that should not be ignored, even when they do not allow the building of models. Policies are generally assumed to have *immediate* and clearly *quantified* and *quantifiable* effects. However, in the real world, lags always exist, and they can be of different and unknown length.

There are also results that are not predictable at the time the policy changes are made, especially but not only when the policies generate major changes on distributional, and not just on allocational, grounds. These are the changes that will be stressed in this book. Economists should pay more attention to these possibilities and not ignore them.

This book will focus mainly on long-term developments and on relationships that are often not easy to subject to quantitative, precise estimations. It will cover three, somewhat distinct, though partly overlapping, periods. The first is the period from around the early or mid-nineteenth century until the 1920s. The second is the period from the Great Depression, in the 1930s, until the 1970s. The third is the post-1970s period, until the Great Recession in 2008–2009, with also some comments on the most recent years.

The years after the Great Recession have characteristics of their own, including, most recently, the impact of the COVID-19 pandemic on the economy, the great increases in public debt and public spending that accompanied the pandemic both in the United States and other countries, and, more recently, the advent of the war in Ukraine and the sudden return of high inflation.

The characteristics and the long-term impact of these recent phenomena are difficult to define or to forecast at this time. They may take different future forms or directions. For this reason, they will receive less direct attention in this study.

During the above three periods, the countries' governments played distinctly different roles for a variety of reasons, including because some important aspects of the economies and of the market were changing significantly. See Summers (2013) on some of these changes in the past four decades, and Tanzi (2011) for an early and longer perspective.

The roles that both the government and market played during the above periods were, at times, close to what was needed and, at other times, far from it. This conclusion implies that the harmony that should exist, or that can be expected or hoped to exist, between the role of the market and that of the state at times increases and at other times decreases, leading to inevitable reactions.

This book will deal with what may be, or may have become, the most important question in economics, namely the economic role that the government or, more broadly, the state should play, in countries that are both democratic and that operate with market economies. That role cannot remain unchanged over long periods of time, as some economists seem to believe. The longer some roles are sustained, the more they set in motion forces that will make it more difficult to sustain those roles in the long-term. This is true for both pro-government and libertarian roles.

The emphasis in this book will often be on the United States, but the arguments will have more general implications and the discussion will be more pragmatic and less formal than is the norm in economics books.

What role should the government play, or should have played at given times? How did that role change over time? And why did it change? How closely did it come to match what the market may have needed, in terms of corrections, and what the countries' citizens may have expected the governments to do, in terms of equity, at a particular time? And why has the government economic role become increasingly larger and more complex with the passing of time in countries that have remained largely democracies with market economies?

This book will speculate on some of the above questions, without the hope of being able to answer them in any precise or definitive manner, and with the expectation that other economists may not agree with the answers given to the questions addressed. But raising some of those questions may have its own merit, because they have not been raised in such a direct way but should have been.

The key or the guiding assumption will be that, at any one time, there should be some balance, or some harmony, between the corrections that the market requires from the government and what many citizens expect the government to do. That balance is not likely to require an unchanging government role and a government role is always required in a large community.

There are and previously have been conservative economists, such as the late James Buchanan and others from the School of Public Choice – the School that Buchanan created in the 1960s – who have argued that, at least in the United States, the broad role of the government, including that of local or subnational governments, was established a long time ago by those who wrote the US Constitution. Therefore, the government should continue to be guided faithfully by those constitutional principles, unless they have been formally modified by constitutional amendments, which are very difficult to make given the institutional set up that was also created a long time ago. In their views, the role of the state should not change in any significant way, even to reflect major structural, economic, technological, and social changes that inevitably take place in the real world and will continue to take place.

The above conservative fundamentalism has continued to have many followers who have viewed any new governmental intervention with suspicion, even when such intervention would save many lives – as would, for example, restrictions on buying guns, a right protected by the US constitution. In the case of guns, the Pew Research Center has reported that, in 2020, 45,222 persons were killed by guns in the United States, and the related costs are $557 billion dollars a year. Clearly this individual freedom has a high social cost.

There are others economists and plain citizens who believe that a market and a society require more, and possibly frequent, changes to better reflect the preferences and the needs of the current generations, not of the generations when the constitutions were drafted, at times centuries ago. For example, the need for individuals to have guns was obviously different two or more centuries ago when most US citizens lived in largely rural settings.

Other economists and informed citizens believe that the government should adjust its role whenever necessary, to correct for changing "market failures" and for developmental changes, which in their view might include the failure of not generating full employment with stable prices, of not creating a reasonable and a broadly or socially-acceptable income distribution, and sustaining an environmental balance that will allow a continuation of life on earth in the future. New scientific evidence may also suggest changes in regulations, as in the impacts of smoking on health and the use of dirty fuels on the environment.

Many economists have continued to pay more attention to the technical concept of allocation of resources and short-term *efficiency*, as defined in traditional "price theory" textbooks, than to the more ambiguous and less precisely defined concepts of *equity and sustainability*, which some economists continue to consider based on *value judgment* and not on *scientific* principles.

The change toward a more "scientific-based" economics, to distinguish it from sociology, came especially after 1870, in part as a consequence of the "Marginalist Revolution in Economics," a revolution that tried to establish boundaries on what should be "economic science" (see Winch, 1972). The marginalist revolution made interpersonal comparisons "unscientific." As a consequence it prevented the comparison of incomes between individuals. These comparisons could not be addressed given the rules of the "science" of economics. This view remained popular until the Great Depression in the 1930s, when it started to be challenged by some. It is still popular today among conservative groups.

However, equity was and has continued to be important to most people. It is especially important for people who live in urban communities where different standards of living are easily observable and where they can and do influence social relations. Equity has become more important with the passing of time, as societies have become more urbanized and as the media have spread more information on the standards of living of different classes. The goods consumed by the upper classes are now advertised for everyone to see. When inequality exceeds certain limits and becomes significant in a society, history teaches us that violence often follows, and it can become the "great leveler" (see Scheidel, 2017).

Attention to equity cannot be ignored by relying on the argument used by some economists that such attention requires a value judgment, while the pursuit of efficiency requires only scientifically based analyses. This misses the point that, in a fundamental way, the concept of efficiency is also based on a value judgment. This is surely the case with the Pareto optimum, a criterium that was broadly accepted and used in welfare economics; or with the definition of *absolute* poverty, that is still widely used today in comparing countries' standards of living. Both dismiss the importance of *relative* incomes and focus on *absolute* incomes, as they are defined, or as they are measured, by current prices, which, in turn, are partly influenced by the existing income distributions. Different income distributions would often lead to different relative prices.

In a rich society, some individuals or families can feel poor even when they have more to eat and a better place to live than people centuries ago. Relative income matters, and the existence of super rich individuals in a society, individuals who today travel in private jets or private yachts, accentuates the differences that exist in the income distributions. This is especially the case in modern societies where the media report on and advertise the habits of the superrich, making the rest of the population feel poorer.

In 1949, James Duesenberry, then an important and highly regarded professor of economics at Harvard University, published a book that gave importance to the relative income position of individuals, in determining their marginal propensity to consume. He theorized that, the lower was the *relative* income position of individuals or families, as opposed to their *absolute* income, the higher would be the marginal propensity to consume out of their incomes. Vice versa, the higher was the relative income of individuals, the higher would be their rate of saving. These behaviors would tend to make the income distribution less even over time and to perpetuate inequality. Available recent statistics, such as the World Inequality Report, 2022 (p. 95) still strongly support Duesenberry's theory.

Poverty cannot be considered just an absolute concept but must be considered a relative one, and the distribution of income, through a "demonstration effect," determines the behavior of consumers, and thus the growth of the economy. Because of its impact on accumulated saving, it also determines the future income distribution.

Equity and efficiency cannot be sharply compartmentalized, as they, often, have been by economists. The position of an individual, or of a family, in the distribution of income is an important factor in determining the saving rates (and the opportunity) faced by different individuals and society. Saving rates are important in determining social mobility.

In the years that followed the publication of Duesenberry's book, the relative income hypothesis was considered important and highly plausible, and it was endorsed and used in some studies (for example, in Tanzi, 1965). (Disclosure: Duesenberry had been one of my professors at Harvard, in the early 1960s). However, in spite of its high plausibility, that hypothesis disappeared in later years, displaced by the less plausible "permanent income hypothesis," advanced by Milton Friedman (see Frank, 2005).

This result was probably due to the rising popularity of Milton Friedman in the 1970s, or perhaps because the relative income hypothesis had relied on sociological or psychological concepts, rather than on purely economic ones such as permanent income. Economists have always struggled in making interpersonal comparisons, so many have refrained from making them (see, also, Palley, 2008).

The views of economists (more than those of normal citizens, who have less precise information but more spontaneous reactions) have oscillated, over the years, between the tendency to see the government as an enemy of a market considered broadly efficient, as economists define efficiency, to that of seeing the government as a possible close replacement for the market, or even as a possible solution for most of the social and economic problems that citizens face. See on this the early debate between Seligman and Nearing in 1922.

The first view was dominant among classical, laissez faire economists, especially during the nineteenth century, when the alternative to laissez faire was mercantilism, that is *excessive* and *arbitrary* government intervention, as it had been in France and other places. Many economists made a dogma of the laissez faire philosophy, which in their view would reduce the governments' arbitrary interventions (see, for example, Bastiat, 1864). Some broadly laissez faire views continue to influence many economists and politicians today.

The alternative view, as especially promoted by Karl Marx and his followers, played a role in experiments with central planning in the twentieth century, in Russia and the Soviet Union countries, and later in China and other countries. The experiments with socialism did not prove particularly successful, and central planning is now much less popular than it used to be. However, some of the thinking that had accompanied it, in milder socialist versions, has continued to attract many people, and even some economists. Many economists now believe that wise and limited government actions can and must be a useful complement to the work of the free market.

2

Early Views on the Economic Role of the State

Over the centuries, various philosophers, political scientists, and, later, economists have theorized about what the role of governments, or more generally the state, should be in an economy. Their theorizing was inevitably influenced by the experiences that they had with the actual roles that governments had been playing, or had played, at times when governments had rarely been democratic.

The government roles, of course, depended on both the *intentions* of the policymakers, their views of the world, and the economic and political *reality* that the policymakers faced. That reality could prevent governments from pursuing some roles that they might have wished to pursue, but that may have been unrealistic, at those times. In those early years, the economic status of families was still largely based on traditional and largely inherited rights, and not on democratic principles or market performance.

Two centuries ago, Edmund Burke had written that: "one of the finest problems in legislature [is] to determine what the state ought to take upon itself to direct by the public wisdom and what it had to leave with as little influence as possible to individual exertion." A century later, in a lecture that he gave in Berlin, in 1926, Keynes would write that "perhaps the chief task of economists ... is to distinguish ... the Agenda of Government from Non-agenda, and the companion task of Politics is to devise forms of Government within" (Keynes, 1926, p. 40). The role of the state had been a long-term topic of debates, starting at least from the time of the Greek philosophers.

In the distant past, and until Adam Smith's time, *mercantilism* had been the most common policy that governments had adopted.

The concept of mercantilism may be a bit vague to current economists, but a good description of it and of its functions can be found in Max Weber's (1923) *General Economic History*. Some detailed and broader description of the specific features of how mercantilism was applied in France in the seventeenth century can also be found in Solomon (1972). In France, in the seventeenth and much of the eighteenth century, mercantilism was promoted through government regulations. The French government imposed many and some rather unusual and extreme forms of regulations. For example, it regulated the height of buildings in Paris, the size of handkerchiefs that could be sold, and even assigned permits to beggars, permits that specified the street corner where a particular beggar could beg. Some other governments, as for example that of the Kingdom of Sardinia, specified the color in which doors of houses could be painted.

Governments regulated trade and other economic activities of individuals and enterprises. Britain followed some forms of mercantilism, as was indicated by Adam Smith, but it did it in a less rigid form than France. This difference can be seen by comparing Paris, with its architectural regularity, and London, with its lack of it.

In 1613, an economist from the then Kingdom of Naples, named Antonio Serra, published a book that provided a rather precise and detailed description of mercantilist policies related to trading activities. In his monumental *History of Economic Analysis*, Schumpeter (1954) would describe Serra's book as the very first book ever written that could claim to be an authentic *economics* book, in a modern sense, rather than just a philosophical treatise.

In Serra's time the wealth of a country was measured mainly by the quantity of gold and silver that the sovereign had available. This was the wealth that could be used for fighting wars, for supporting sovereigns, and for other national purposes. It was the kind of wealth that had made Spain rich and powerful at that time, due to the gold and silver coming from its American colonies.

In the absence of gold and silver mines in a country, or in conquered territories, such wealth could be accumulated mainly through trade, by limiting imports, through import duties and other government-imposed restrictions, while giving incentives and support to exporters. At that time payments for imports and receipts for exports were settled in gold and silver, which were the means of exchange. Therefore, the balance of payment largely determined the wealth, in gold and silver, that a country had available.

Some may recognize that Serra's policy was broadly the same one that was strongly recommended, in the 1950s and 1960s, to Argentina and other Latin American countries, by Raul Prebisch, then an influential Argentina economist. The declared objective of Prebisch, however, was not that of accumulating gold and silver for governments, but that of promoting industrial development in those countries, at a time when industrialization was seen by many economists as a necessary precondition for economic development. If a country wanted to develop into a developed country, it had to industrialize. One way to promote industrialization was to impose obstacles to the import of many products, in order to provide implicit subsidies to local producers, replacing the imported products with local production. That is how Argentina ended up producing, in those years, US-designed cars that had not been produced in the United States for many years. The view was that, with high enough import duties, a country could produce almost anything. Of course, the costs of production could become very high, making a country poor rather than rich.

In Max Weber's book, published in 1923, almost three centuries after Serra's book, he explained that mercantilism had been part of the formation of the "rational" state and that "modern capitalism" could flourish only in a "rational" state, a state that was capable of guarantying *consistent* policies to private enterprises. Modern states had come into existence only in relatively recent centuries, and in some countries, such as England and France, earlier than in others. They had not existed, as such, in the distant past. Mercantilism had been the first expression of a modern *capitalist* state and a road to it.

As Weber put it, mercantilism had

consist[ed] in carrying the point of view of capitalistic industry in politics; the state [was] handled as if it consisted exclusively of capitalistic entrepreneurs. External economic policy rest[ed] on the principle of taking any advantage of the [foreign] opponent, importing at the lowest price and selling much higher. Hence mercantilism signifie[d] the development of the state as a political power, which [was] to be done by increasing the tax paying power of the population.

(Weber, 1923, pp. 255–256)

Weber added that: "England is distinctly the original home of Mercantilism. The first traces of the application of mercantilist principles are found [in England] in the year 1381" (Weber, 1923).

A century and a half after Serra, and at the very beginning of the Industrial Revolution, the Scottish economist Adam Smith (1776) would present a different and more utilitarian, or more modern, definition of the "wealth of the nations," in a book that would become the most influential and famous book in the history of economics, appropriately titled, *The Wealth of Nations.*

In what was then a novel and revolutionary view, Smith identified the wealth of nations not with the amount of gold and silver owned by a country but with the wellbeing of the individuals who lived and operated in it. The wealth was in the hands of the citizens and not in the hands of the state. There was, thus, an implicit acceptance, on the part of Adam Smith, that the wellbeing had to originate and to be found among the population, rather than being the gold and silver concentrated in the safes of the state and largely in the hands of the sovereigns.

Smith explained that the individuals of a community, acting in their own interest and without the need for any government to guide them, had incentives to produce what other members of the community needed and would want to buy. Each member had the incentive to sell to others and to buy from others, what he or she and others did not produce, but needed. Ricardo would later extend this concept to the trade between England and Portugal, introducing a global dimension to the principle (see Ricardo, 1817).

Smith added that an "invisible hand" would somehow coordinate the actions of the individuals, without any need for the government to play a direct role. For the first time, Adam Smith had proposed a philosophy of *laissez faire*, a philosophy that would become popular and would acquire many followers during the nineteenth century, especially among individuals who had some training in the new and developing field of economics. Economists would develop the theoretical underpinnings of the laissez faire economics that Smith had advanced. And laissez faire would play a fundamental and useful role during the industrial revolution.

The industrial revolution would significantly be promoted by laissez faire, even when governments would continue to interfere to varying degrees in some economic activities. Religion would also play a role in the economic developments in those years (see Friedman, 2021).

Perhaps it could be mentioned at this point that the industrial revolution would create many needs for new energy, which initially would come from running water and from the use of coal and later from oil and gas. These new energy sources would lead to great increases in average incomes over the years. In the long-term this would create the problem of global warming that has become increasingly problematic in recent times.

While laissez faire is often identified with Adam Smith's work, the term did not originate with him. Rather, it had a much earlier origin, in France, during the time when Jean Baptiste Colbert was the powerful finance minister of Louis XIV, the then king of France. At that time mercantilism was the prevalent economic philosophy that guided France and other countries.

One day Colbert invited several leading French merchants to discuss possible ways in which the state could help them in their commercial activities that would increase France's possessions of gold and silver, an increase that the country badly needed. During the discussion, and in response to Colbert's question on how the state could help them in their activities, one of the merchants present, by the name of Legendre, commented that the best help that the government could provide them was by simply staying out of their way and their activities. As he put it, in French, by *nous laissez faire*, by "letting us do our things." That was the origin of the term. As we saw earlier, the state had been interfering in many activities in which it had no legitimate business to intervene, and it was often allocating monopoly power on some activities to specific, favored merchants.

Adam Smith used the term "invisible hand" briefly and only in passing. However, that term would be often used, over the years by various commentators, as an argument that the government should have almost no role to play in the market, and that it should simply "stay out of the activities of private agents." These commentators still expected the government to perform its important role of protecting the private properties of citizens and the personal safety of individuals and, of course, of defending the country from invasion from other countries, and providing essential institutions and infrastructures. For all these activities governments would inevitably need some revenues through taxes. However, the payment of these was often resisted.

A careful reading of all of Adam Smith's writings, including his other important book, *The Theory of Moral Sentiments* (1759), conveys a more nuanced message than implied by the common view of laissez faire. Smith did not live in the abstract world of theoretical economics and he had his feet firmly placed on the ground (see Buchan, 2006). He was a keen observer of the reality that surrounded him and he was fully aware that market operators could try, and often did try, to take advantage of their customers, when they could. They did this by organizing "cartels" and by other means that allowed them to extract higher profits from their economic operations. He was also aware that there were some essential infrastructures and some services that later would be called public goods, that only governments could provide. When possible, the infrastructures could be built by private interests that could charge fees for their use, as was the case with turnpikes that significantly reduced the number of hours that it took to go to London from other major British cities.

Smith also realized that, in all communities, there are some individuals who, because of circumstances or personal handicaps, might not be able to produce and sell anything that others wanted, including their labor. These individuals might not have any income to support their essential needs. In the absence of some assistance, that might come from other members of large families, from charitable and religious institutions, or from the government, these individuals would be forced to become beggars or criminals or simply starve. These were prospects that a caring community would and should not accept and should not ignore.

As large families started to disappear and religious institutions reduced their role, the government would have to assume a larger role in filling this need. Since Elizabeth I, England had had some poor laws aimed at providing some assistance to very poor individuals who were not able to feed themselves. These laws had filled the role that in the past had been played by convents and other religious institutions before the religious separation from the Papacy.

In conclusion, while Adam Smith recognized the beneficial role that small and noninterfering governments could provide to the work of free markets, and to the welfare of its citizens, he also recognized the need for some regulatory function by the governments, and for some governmental assistance to individuals in need and not able to provide for themselves. He also elaborated some basic rules related to the imposition of taxes and was against the use of public debt by governments.

The limited functions of the state would be justified even in the largely laissez faire environment that was contemplated and favored by Adam Smith. This meant that equity could not be left out of the equation, and that if the market did not provide it, the government should. Smith was in favor of a free society, but of a society that was a decent and caring one. Such a society might not arise spontaneously in an extreme laissez faire environment, He wanted to create incentives for free individuals, not only for them to do better economically, but also to act better, reflecting some altruistic community notions. He gave significant importance to "empathy" (see Muller, 1993) for elaborations of these points, and especially the last chapter of Smith's *The Theory of Moral Sentiment*.

It should be added that Smith's theorizing was conditioned by the environment in which he lived, one then made up of inherited privileges and some mostly small economic activities. The market he referred to, with some exceptions, was then prevalently local, and the market exchanges that took place were mostly repeated exchanges, among individuals who knew one another and focused on material goods rather than services. Transparency could be assumed in this market and competitive prices were important in the exchanges.

This society would dramatically change over the next centuries and during the Industrial Revolution, when factories that could host thousands of workers under the same roof started to be built, leading to the obvious question of whether what might have been good in Smith's time would still be good in a different environment. When the weather changes, should one wear the same clothes or change clothes? This was and has remained the key question.

3

Laissez Faire and the Industrial Revolution

The belief in the dogma of the free market took hold in the early part of the nineteenth century and many economists came to believe in its validity. It should be noted that they saw laissez faire as a desirable alternative to the then prevalent mercantilism, as had been clearly seen by Adam Smith, not as an alternative to efficient government policies, which probably did not exist at that time.

To give an example of the extent to which laissez faire became a dogma or a religion for some economists, in 1853, the most famous Italian economist of the time, Francesco Ferrara, who was a professor of economics at the University of Torino and a prolific writer and firm believer in the evil of state intervention in economic activities, wrote that the use of import duties by the US government in those years was "a sin as grave as that of slavery."

The United States would commit the first of these sins during much of the laissez faire period, for the rest of the nineteenth century, and it would continue committing the second sin until 1865, when the Civil War, or the War between the States, came to an end, and slavery was abolished. While the United States stopped committing the second sin in 1865, the fist sin had become even more sinful during the Civil War, when the Union government, in desperate need for public revenue to fight the war, had sharply raised import duties. It had also introduced, for the first time, a temporary income tax (see Lowenstein, 2022). A permanent income tax would be introduced in 1913.

The American Civil War significantly increased the power of the US Federal government, from the very limited role that it had played in the past (mainly delivering the mail, some defense spending, and doing relatively little else), at a time when individuals living in the United States had considered their connection to the specific "states" in which they lived far more important than their connection to the Federal government. The process of unification of countries, as happened in Italy and Germany in those decades, would generate similar results. It would increase the importance of national or central governments and of national policies.

Over time, national governments have greater need than local governments for public resources, because they must provide *national* public goods and services and promote *national* objectives, which in growing economies tend to increase. In the United States, the unification after the Civil War would involve the incorporation of the huge West, after the wars with Mexico and with the many "Indian tribes" that had considered those lands their territories. Wars also increase the importance of central governments.

During laissez faire, various countries would continue to use import duties as revenue sources and development tools, as they had done during the years of mercantilism. Governments would also continue to intervene with regulations and other tools, including import duties, to assist specific industries, such as steel, railroads, or, in the United States, even Coca Cola (see Taussig, 1892). The US government also engaged in the large distribution of the lands acquired in the West to individuals.

The pressures coming from vested interests did not disappear during the laissez faire period, as they would not disappear, much later, during the years of market fundamentalism in the 1980s onward. They would take different forms. Laissez faire as an economic philosophy has remained a dogma for many economists. At times, it became a convenient excuse for governments when they did not want to do certain things, such as helping some individuals in need, as the English government failed to do during the Irish potato famine in the late 1840s (see Tanzi, 2022).

By the middle of the nineteenth century the interests of the newly emerging class that was associated with the Industrial Revolution was pushing for changes in the traditional government political structure. The at times violent demonstrations that had characterized the year 1848, often described as "la revolution des clercs," had been led by these new groups.

By the late nineteenth century, the Industrial Revolution had advanced enough to have radically changed the mostly rural world that had existed a century earlier, when Adam Smith had lived. By that time "... manufacturing had shifted from the home to the factory and from the hand to the machine," and "concentration of industry [had] followed"

(Faulkner, 1951, p. 3). The economic power of some individuals had increased, because of their own effort and their new activities. The economic and, increasingly, the social landscape had also changed, and modern states had come into existence (see Weitz, 2019).

The change had created the need to adjust some policies and pay more attention to the objective of equity, which had become more pressing as the more numerous factory workers were acquiring some powers by starting to organize. While some political reforms had been introduced during the nineteenth century, more fundamental ones would have to wait until the first decade of the twentieth century, and especially during the 1930s, in response to the Great Depression.

Some economic historians, such as Carlo Cipolla, have written that laissez faire prevented or retarded some public expenditure, such as the financing of general public education, that could have increased economic growth and the incomes of those who had not had the means to buy education with their own resources. One can also theorize that there must have been some minimum level of public spending in infrastructure, for example on roads, that would have increased mobility and economic growth, if it had been met.

While too high tax levels might become obstacles to growth, too low levels may also have a negative effect on growth. The early literature on economic development of less developed countries had stressed this possibility. In today's rich countries there had been relatively little growth, until tax levels and the needed public spending that they financed started to increase in the later part of the Industrial Revolution.

The reforms that began to be introduced in the early part of the twentieth century and especially after the 1930s in the United Kingdom, the United States and some other countries, were aimed at reducing the gap that had developed between the actual and, what many economists had come to consider, the needed role of the state. They aimed to reduce the gap and bring some harmony between the two roles.

By the end of the nineteenth century, that gap had become particularly large in terms of social and economic needs and in terms of equity. The reforms that had been introduced before the First World War and in the 1930s, and that were introduced especially after the war, would also bring some needed changes in the operations of the market that was showing signs of distortions, as for example by reducing the role of monopolies.

In the decades that followed the publication of *The Wealth of Nations* (Smith, 1776), the Industrial Revolution would, first slowly and then at an accelerating pace, transform the economic and social world that had existed. The traditional nobles – who in the past had owned and inherited many properties, had lived on rents, had much of the political power, and to a large extent had determined the output of many artisans who had been producing items made mostly for them – would lose ground to the newly emerging bourgeoisie. This change would be due to both the effects of the French Revolution and, later and more importantly, to the maturing of the Industrial Revolution (see Ashton, 1948).

The Industrial Revolution mostly affected the North of the United States, with little effect on the agricultural South. That revolution would prove to be the most radical of all revolutions because it would change, radically and permanently, the world that had existed. It would also make the need for a larger government role in the economy obvious.

The increasingly powerful bourgeoisie, made up of newly rich industrialists (and a few earlier nobles), came into existence and challenged and, over the years, replaced the old aristocracies, not only in political and economic power but also in determining what a wider market would produce and what role the government should play. These new rich owed their wealth and their newly acquired power to their own effort more than to government's concessions.

The output of highly talented artisans, that in the past had been directed mainly toward satisfying the refined tastes of the nobles, would, to a large extent, be replaced by the mass produced, less refined and sophisticated, but much cheaper and more convenient, output made by machines. Machines would progressively replace the output of previously self-employed workers and, to a lesser extent, of servants.

The new rich would start using their wealth to establish new links and new networks with other rich people and to get favorable policies and regulations from the governments, as elites normally do and as nobles had done in the past. Corruption of governments would play an important part in those years. Wealthy people are generally not happy to operate under rules that restrict their activities and their actions, and the new rich individuals were no different.

In this transition from the old, feudal world to the new industrializing and modern world, some of the talented artisans, who had operated before the Industrial Revolution, and had at times produced outstanding works of art, architecture, and even engineering (such as magnificent musical instruments, and marvelous mechanical clocks that had required outstanding mechanical skills) would lose their functions. What the Industrial Revolution had brought was cheaper energy, energy that could more easily replace the manual worker but not the artistic talent of many workers.

The mechanical clocks that some artisans had produced before the Industrial Revolution had been particularly important in providing some regularity and some rhythm to the activities of town people, a regularity that had been far less important in the rural areas. In many European towns, mechanical clocks had been placed on bell towers, where they could be easily seen by the cities' citizens, most of whom did not have clocks. The clocks would instruct them when to go to some activities, including the opening and closing of shops, theater performances, religious ceremonies, and others.

The introduction of clocks, by giving more value to time, would be important in increasing productivity, especially in the cities. The use of time would be as important as that of cheap energy for the Industrial Revolution and for the coming of the modern world. When the mechanical clocks had been installed on bell towers, where everyone who lived in a city could see them, they would become good examples of what public finance economists would call "public goods."

The second half of the nineteenth century saw the rise of "Big Business," both in Europe and in the United States, a rise associated with the creation of large, unregulated, and untaxed enterprises that often operated as monopolies. These enterprises would increase output but distort the market. They would generate huge incomes and increasing political power for the few people who owned them.

At that time the ownership of the enterprises had not been widely socialized, as it would be in later years, with the creation of the corporate form of ownership and of many shareholders. In those years, the owners of the large enterprises were, generally, single, with a few partnerships. The members of the new elite must have felt that they were ready to run and change the world that had existed, especially at a time when the nobles were losing, or had lost, some of their inherited privileges. The new elite would acquire increasing political powers and start creating connections among its members.

The new industrial enterprises would become progressively larger. They would require new enormous buildings to accommodate their many workers and would be concentrated in places where energy sources (initially mostly coal and running water) were located. They would hire thousands of workers and produce large outputs in few places, making these areas increasingly urban.

The workers who found work in these enterprises needed to live nearby, in order to be able to commute and report daily, at a specified time, to and from the factories where they worked on daily contracts, for twelve hours a day, six days a week, at wages that were very low, and in jobs where accidents were far from rare. They could easily be fired when they were not needed, or for any other reason, and they lost their wages if they were ill.

In those years, there were still no formal safety nets for the workers and their families, and young children were part of the labor force, often being used in mines and other unhealthy and dangerous jobs. The children also worked for many hours a day for very low wages. Not surprisingly, average life expectancy was low, generally less than forty years, so few reached old age.

The gradual passage from mercantilism to laissez faire had transferred much power from the state to the owners of the enterprises who, because of their wealth, often acquired influence on the governing bodies In several countries and places, such as New York and Chicago, corruption as a form of influencing policies and softening some regulations became a common factor. For many workers, especially those who had been self-employed before the Industrial Revolution, the laissez faire policies had not led to improvement in their standards of living but to unemployment and loss of income.

This situation would contribute to the creation of a class consciousness among industrial workers, the so-called proletariat, a consciousness that had not existed among rural workers in the past. Industrial workers increasingly resented their economic conditions and their low social status, especially when they compared them with those of their employers. More equality and better working conditions became an important objective for many of them, more than it had been in the old rural world.

Over time, some workers began to organize and to push for higher wages and better working conditions (see Loria, 1903). An increasing share of workers would be attracted to newly forming labor unions. These associations were strongly opposed by employers and laissez faire economists, because they were seen as interfering with the free market by raising wages and making it more difficult for enterprises to fire workers.

There would be the beginning of many strikes which were considered illegal. With the passing of time, the strikes would become progressively more violent, in the United States more than in Europe. European workers, such as those in France, Germany, and Italy, would be increasingly attracted to socialist or even to communist ideas.

At the same time the creation of the large enterprises and the concentration of wages and output in a few places were creating the potential for alternative and higher sources of tax revenues for future governments, should the social and political environment change enough to make higher tax revenue desirable and politically feasible.

As the nineteenth century progressed, and the Industrial Revolution matured, the economic and social situation changed at a faster pace. Conditions were being created for governments to add to the tax bases that had been available to them in the past (which had been mainly import duties, a few limited excises, and some taxes on real property), to include the far more productive tax bases of income and general sales. These new and larger bases would make it possible to significantly raise the existing tax levels and, thus, finance a different and larger role of the state, as would happen in the twentieth century. Naturally, laissez faire economists would see this as interfering in the work of the free economy and in its natural development.

During the nineteenth century, the populations of many countries increased significantly, especially in the cities, while rural areas generally became less populated. In the United States the total population rose from around 30 million in 1850 to around 70 million in 1900, due in significant part to immigration from Europe and Asia.

The extended families, that had lived mainly in rural villages, and that had provided a primitive but real safety net for individual members who might have needed help, including the old, the very young, and the invalid, broke up, as members of working ages moved away, to go where the new and often distant jobs had become available. Soon the large extended families would become past institutions and the safety nets that they had provided disappeared.

This would create a need for alternative safety nets, but it would take a long time before the informal safety nets that had existed in the past would be replaced by new, formal ones. The formal ones would require new policies and the willingness to create them. In the meantime, the past community spirit that had existed in rural villages was being eroded and more individualistic attitudes (apart from the growing class consciousness among the workers) would become common.

Many of the individuals who in the past had worked in traditional occupations (as shoemakers, blacksmiths, carpenters, bakers, tailors, and other traditional jobs), operating from their cottages mostly in rural villages, were progressively left without work, when their output was replaced by cheaper products, produced by machines (Ashton, 1948; Mokyr, 1990)

There was also less need for agricultural workers, because of the higher productivity, the opening of new agricultural areas in parts of the world, and the role that railroads and steamboats played in transporting grain, wheat, meat, and other products from newly opened agricultural areas in Argentina, Brazil, Australia, and the American Mid-West to the new cities with large populations. Thus, the proportion of agricultural workers in advanced countries fell.

In catholic countries, religious organizations, financed by past or current donations from wealthier individuals, continued to provide some minimum, charitable assistance to those in need. In protestant countries, however, there was more of a tendency "to see every poor person as work-shy or even as a criminal," and it was assumed that assistance was against the spirit of a capitalist system (Weber, 1923, p. 257; see also Weber, 2002, for the assumed connection between Protestantism and Capitalism).

In several countries, pressures started to build on governments, that by that time had become more democratic, to provide some assistance to "deserving" individuals and to families in need, to begin to regulate monopolies, and to increase tax levels to allow governments to more easily pursue these potential responsibilities. The relative importance of equity was growing, compared with that of efficiency. In 1919, the creation of the International Labor Office might be seen as a response to the Progressive Age and the creation of the League of Nations, which the United States did not join, was also an indication of some global concern about equity.

By the end of the nineteenth century, the general appeal of laissez faire had started to decline, even among nonsocialist economists and citizens (see Faulkner, 1951). This was happening at a time when governments were becoming more democratic because of the growing proportions of populations, including women, who would acquire the right to vote in the early decades of the twentieth century in the United States and the United Kingdom.

4

The Beginning of Economic Reforms

The nineteenth century had seen some reforms but more in the political than in the economic areas. It had also witnessed the major economic changes that the Industrial Revolution was bringing. At the beginning of the nineteenth century, the countries had still mostly been rural and, in Europe, societies were still somewhat feudal, even after the French Revolution and its impact on several countries.

The nineteenth century would see various important political and constitutional reforms that widened the civil rights of many citizens. For that reason, some historians have called it "the age of reform" (see Woodward, 2000). However, the nineteenth-century reforms had been mainly *political*, including the widening of the right to vote. They had not been, more strictly, reforms in the economic area and, during those years, the Industrial Revolution had been changing economies and social relations in some fundamental ways.

The nineteenth-century reforms made some countries more democratic and gave more freedom, especially to those who were promoting the Industrial Revolution. However, until late in the century, there were still few reforms aimed at increasing workers' *economic* claims versus their employers or toward the state. The reforms aimed at increasing the right of workers vis-à-vis their employers had been limited. The Bismarck's pension reforms had been a major exception that would have much influence with time in Germany and beyond.

During the nineteenth century, and especially during the second part of the century, two economic and sharply contrasting schools of thought had acquired many followers. The first had been the *laissez faire* school, briefly discussed in Chapter 3. This had been popular with classical economists and was followed by the more conservative *marginal revolu-tion*, increasingly popular with many *neoclassical* economists, after 1870s. The second influential school had been *socialism*.

Socialism was not a unified school but it had several expressions and came in various versions, some more restrictive or more radical than others. Its influence would increase especially in the second part of the century, when the views of Karl Marx and of his followers would become predominant.

Both schools had implications about the fairness of the existing economic system and about what should or should not be done about the way that system was working, which had been developing during the Industrial Revolution. By the middle of the nineteenth century, the laissez faire ideology had become increasingly popular with economists, had been refined by mathematicians, and had acquired followers outside the economic profession, especially among wealthier individuals who liked its conclusions.

By that time, economics had become an established academic field, taught in many universities. Classical economists saw the merits of *laissez faire* in the *allocation* of economic resources and in the promotion of economic growth and "progress," at a time when the Industrial Revolution was going on. Laissez faire had come to be seen as a necessary ingredient for that revolution, that ran the danger of being stopped by Luddites (individuals who had lost their previous occupations because of the advent of machines), socialists, or even governments that wanted to continue with their mercantilist policies.

Extreme and ecologically based, or Darwinian, view of laissez faire, seen as the "survival of the fittest" in ecological systems, were also presented (see Spenser, 1884). At this time many economists were still reacting to the mercantilist policies that some countries had continued to pursue in milder versions, and believed that markets could be efficient if left alone, especially when they compared the laissez faire policies, as they were seen to work in theory, with the likely alternative of government-promoted mercantilist monopolies.

By the second half of the nineteenth century, laissez faire (as later amended by the marginal revolution) had become the preferred school of thought among economists, who strongly praised its liberating quality. What could be more liberating than having the faculty of doing what you wanted, without being limited by inefficient governments and without encountering other constraints, as long as you did not intentionally damage others and as long as you respected a few laws, as John Stuart Mill had written in a famous essay on liberty? (see Mill, 1962).

Laissez faire economists came to see the natural evolution of economic activities in a way that resembled the Darwinian ecological or natural evolution that, by that time, had become popular. Free economic systems came to be seen as ecological systems, with their natural dynamic and with their tendency to develop and, if allowed to do their work, of being capable of developing and leading to a better future *for all citizens* in the long-term, while favoring the "fittest" and the harder working and enterprising, the ones that deserved to be favored.

Laissez faire was also, clearly, a less socially unsettling alternative for the existing societies, which had well-established property rights, than socialism, in addition to being a better alternative to mercantilism. Therefore, laissez faire became the preferred choice, not only among economists but also among many better-to-do people, who, at that time, were still mostly individuals who had the right to vote, in countries that were becoming more democratic. The philosophy of laissez faire also influenced some governments. This may have been more so in the United Kingdom and United States than in countries on the European continent.

In the United States and United Kingdom, it was felt that economics in general and especially public finance, should remain focused on the provision of private goods and on the application of free prices to the economic exchanges among citizens. Public finance as a field of study remained relatively underdeveloped in the Anglo-Saxon countries compared to some continental European countries. With its actions, the government should not distort economic choices, as the marginal revolution would stress. No theory of public goods developed in the Anglo-Saxon countries, as they did in some continental European countries.

In Italy, the "Scienza delle Finanze," the school that had developed in the second part of the nineteenth century, became a major school on its own. It had begun to speculate about a larger role of the government. That "School" would later influence the thinking of James Buchanan, who spent a sabbatical year in Italy in the mid-1950s. Buchanan would later acknowledge that "the Scienza delle Finance" had influenced his thinking.

It could be mentioned that Locke ([1690] 1939, pp. 6–7) had already called attention to the existence of externalities that could reduce the liberty of individuals, a liberty that was assumed in a laissez faire environment. Externalities and public goods would later receive more attention, first by Pigou, and then by Samuelson, but they would remain difficult topics to deal with for libertarian economists, who continued to minimize the role that the state should play in the economy.

The indifference of laissez faire to questions of income and wealth distributions, at a time when those distributions were becoming less egalitarian because of the Industrial Revolution, would start to worry a small but increasing number of individuals, and not just socialists. Those worries would lead some critics (as, for example, the Swedish dramatist August Strindberg) to comment, in an often cited comment and somewhat ironically, that, in those years, economics had become "the science by which the rich remained the rich."

Laissez faire had become the preferred choice for a specific class, especially the growing capitalist class, and for the class of those who had inherited wealth. However, growing worries about equity aspects, which were echoed in literary works by Dickens, Zola, Hugo, and others, were leading an increasing number of individuals to socialist alternatives.

Laissez faire economists, which were closely linked to the developing capitalist system, continued to show little interest in the distribution of income and wealth that resulted from laissez faire policies and from wealth inheritance but much interest in technical questions related to market *equilibrium* and to the *optimal* use of the scarcely available resources. The optimal use of resources was believed to maximize the output from the limited resources available and, gradually and progressively, to increase the wellbeing of everyone, thus leading to greater future welfare. This conclusion would occasionally be criticized but it would retain its central importance in the economic thinking of the time.

An increasing number of individuals, some with strong mathematical skills (Walras, Pareto, Barone, and others), were being attracted to the new field of economics and helped to formalize the main principles of classical economics. This made economics look increasingly *scientific*, compared to how it had been in the past and it would be under socialism, even when socialism called itself "scientific" and developed some "deterministic laws" that were supposed to indicate how capitalistic economies would naturally evolve toward some forms of socialism. See Marx ([1867] 1906), Seligman (1907), and, later, Schumpeter (1942) for some elaboration of this thesis.

5

On Resource Allocation, Optimality, and Equity

The principles of economics that developed in the nineteenth century, guided by laissez faire principles, which later incorporated those of the marginal revolution, accepted the distributional results of the work of the free market, and, implicitly, accepted the existing social arrangements as to the ownership and inheritance of property, the current taxing, or lack of it, of income and wealth, and the level of industrial wages. Therefore, it largely ignored questions of equity and distribution of income and wealth, accepting the market outcomes as the natural legitimate results of the economic process of evolution. In this process of evolution, population control was thought to play an important role in the determination of real wages and in the Malthusian problem. The greater was the growth of the population, the lower would have to be real wages and the standards of living of workers.

The concept of Pareto Optimum, a concept that had been developed by the Italian economist Vilfredo Pareto around the end of the nineteenth century, came to be widely endorsed by many economists. In some ways it represented what J. S. Mill had called *summum bonum* (see Mill, 2004, p. 251). The Pareto Optimum stated that the *addition* to the legitimate income of anyone in a community would be welfare enhancing as long as nobody else would be made worse off, in *absolute* terms. This conclusion was assumed to hold regardless of whether those who gained from a given policy were the super-rich or the very poor. The Pareto Optimum had strong distributional and allocational implications and its principle came to be applied to policies in general.

Marginalist, utilitarian principles, that stressed that the utilities of different individuals were not comparable, were used to endorse the validity of the Pareto Optimum. These marginalist principles would not support the taxation of wealthier individuals with progressive taxes or the redistribution of income through spending programs, as Adolf Wagner had been advocating in the concluding years of the nineteenth century.

The Pareto Optimum principle led to the support of "optimal taxes," which were taxes, such as poll taxes, or excises levied on essential goods, such as salt. These were taxes that could not be avoided, or shifted, by the taxpayer. Therefore, they did not change the economic behavior of the taxed individuals, or the allocation of resources. Optimal taxes focused all their attention on the substitution effect of taxes, on resource allocation, and on economic efficiency in general. Equity or redistributive consider-ations or the income effects of taxes were ignored.

For the Pareto Optimum, and for the members of the marginalist school, the utilities of different individuals were not comparable and should not be compared. Taking a dollar from a super-rich individual might cause as much discomfort for that individual, if he were a "miser," as taking it from a very poor person who was "ascetic" or "altruistic." These utility comparisons between individuals were simply not allowed by the thinking that came to prevail among laissez faire and classical economists. These comparisons could not be based on *science*, but had to be based on *value judgments*, and the *science of economics* did not allow the use of *unscientific* value judgments. Therefore, income transfers and policy-induced changes in the distributions of income and wealth were not endorsed by laissez faire economics, and redistributive policies con-tinued to receive little if any attention by most economists.

Laissez faire and classical economics assumed that the incomes gener-ated by a well working and efficient national market, a market with clearly established legitimate property rights and a very limited govern-ment role in the economy and made up of individuals acting freely and with full knowledge, were legitimate and fully deserved by those who received them. Therefore, attempts at changing the market-generated income distribution, by transfers through public policies of some income from richer to poorer individuals, was not justified, on both economic and ethical grounds.

Forced redistribution could have negative consequences on the alloca-tion of resources and on the performances of the economies. Taxes were widely seen as economically damaging, as many economists have con-tinued to see them (see Adams, 1998). If market imperfections led to unfair income distributions, it was the imperfections that should be corrected, not the income distributions.

As the income distributions became more unequal with the maturing of the Industrial Revolution, the assumption that the incomes generated by the market were always fully deserved started to be challenged. The welfare states, that would be created after the Second World War, would aim at promoting less unequal income distributions and standards of living and at providing some safety nets to individuals and families.

Historically, the concept of economic "justice" has had different definitions (see, for example, Mill, 2004, p. 301). Socialists had flatly refused to accept the view that economic justice could be different from income equality, and they had seen property as being equivalent to "theft." However, a free market might generate different incomes that might be seen as fully deserved and, thus, consistent with some definition of "economic justice."

The other popular school of thought in the nineteenth century had been socialism. Socialism had many proponents and many branches and meanings, and over the nineteenth century had attracted an increasing number of followers, especially and increasingly among the growing number of industrial workers. It had also attracted the attention of a few important, mainstream economists, for example, Barone (1907) and, later, Lange and Taylor (1938) and others, who were intrigued by its theoretical possibilities and who were uncomfortable with the current income inequality. However, classical economists, such as Von Mises, Hayek, and others, and even Keynes, would remain unconvinced by the socialist claims. See Mallock (1908) for an early discussion of views on socialism and the debate between Seligman and Nearing.

The two branches of socialism that could be considered to represent many were: a mild version, hardly a formal *school*, that could be called *Catholic socialism*; and a hard version, that, with the passing of the years, became, increasingly popular, the *Marxist* version, inspired by the writings of Karl Marx.

Catholicism had always stressed the virtue of poverty, and the Christian merit of charity and sharing within a community. There was some sharing of wealth or income, spontaneously or in some organized ways through government policies, as later would be done in welfares states, or as it had been done traditionally through religious and charitable institutions, which often functioned as a proxy for missing government welfare policies. They were financed by donations, which were praised in Catholic societies.

In Catholic society, poverty was not necessarily an absolute measure. One was not poor in an absolute sense. One could be poor or rich in comparison to others, and the richer a person was, the greater was the obligation for some sharing on his/her part. That school was criticized by economists with a Protestant background, who assigned more importance to the action of individuals in the determination of their own standards of living and tended to associate poverty with laziness or other defects.

Both versions of socialism would end up having some applications in the twentieth century. Versions of Catholic socialism probably influenced the welfare states; and the Marxist version found its full application in the centrally planned, communist countries after the 1917 Russian Revolution and after the Second World War.

Until the second half of the nineteenth century it would not have been possible, in any case, for governments to play modern economic roles – roles that required significantly higher public spending – as would be the case later in welfare states, even if the countries' policymakers had wanted to. In those years the governments would not have had the financial resources needed by a role that envisaged much public spending. Given the structure of the economies and of the political power in societies at that time, they could not have been able to raise the needed high tax levels, and they could not have been able to hire the competent bureaucrats needed to supervise and monitor modern economic programs (see Tanzi, 2018b).

Public debt was expensive and difficult to obtain before central banks started changing that reality in the twentieth century. Recourse to debt by governments had generally been considered bad policy by past political leaders, from Napoleon to George Washington, and also by leading economists, including Adam Smith and David Hume. The above difficulty made laissez faire the easier alternative, both politically and administratively, even though it might not necessarily, or always, have been the policy that all governments would have preferred if they had faced different financial and political realities, and most governments continued to violate some of the principles of laissez faire during the nineteenth century.

Until about 1900, the tax and public spending levels had remained relatively low in all countries, generally less than 10 percent of gross domestic product (GDP). In the United States, for example, in 1902, the share of total government spending into GDP was only 7.7 percent (see Mosher and Poland, 1964, p. 157). In spite of the increases during the First World War and the New Deal, the share of taxes remained under 20 percent of GDP until 1940. It is still less than 30 percent of GDP today, a low level by the standards of advanced countries.

The low tax levels in the nineteenth century were barely sufficient to finance the government needs: (a) to sustain the still high expenses of many sovereigns; (b) to cover expenses for defense and for occasional wars; and (c) to cover needs for financing the administration of justice, internal security, and some essential infrastructures, that were increasingly necessary because of the impact of the Industrial Revolution. See Leroy-Beaulieu (1888) for data on earlier years and, for later years, see Tanzi and Schuknecht (2000) and Schuknecht (2020).

After 1900 the share of taxes and public expenses into GDP started rising, first slowly, until the Second World War, and then rapidly, until about 1980. After 1980 the growth slowed down, until the most recent pandemic years, when public spending shot up.

Taxes had been low for several objective reasons:

1. In the early years, few citizens had the right to vote, and those who did have that right were male, property owners, and individuals able to pay the poll taxes. These voters would not have supported higher taxes in democratic countries where their votes counted. In later years the extension of voting rights to low-income individuals and to women led to progressively more support for higher social spending policies, and for higher taxes to finance them, especially when the taxes could be based on the ability to pay, as would be with the progressive taxes on income that were increasingly used.

2. As already explained, the "sociology" or the "reality" of taxation would have made it difficult to collect higher taxes, because the available tax bases had been limited and dispersed. The Industrial Revolution progressively changed that reality (see Tanzi, 2018b).

3. In later years, higher taxes and better and more public schools made it possible for governments to hire better-trained public employees, from the larger pool of educated citizens. These could better administer the social programs.

4. Thinking about allocation and equity started changing, as equity became more important in the increasing number of countries that were becoming more democratic.

6

Beginning of Changes in the Activities of Governments

By the second half of the nineteenth century the process of industrialization had advanced a great deal and major technological, demographic, and social changes had accompanied it. Industrialization had been, in some ways, a democratic process, because it had involved many able citizens from different social backgrounds and not just the privileged few. It started producing many goods that, in the past, had not been available or had been available only through the limited output of talented artisans and in short supply. The better goods had been directed mainly to satisfy the needs or the wishes of rich customers who could afford them.

In assessing the impact of the Industrial Revolution, it should not be forgotten that the period before had produced outstanding musical instruments, very complex mechanical clocks, and other mechanical and artistic marvels. These had been produced in very small supply by highly talented artisans, who could not have mass produced them, because of the time and the talent that it took to make them. What that period had not been able to do was to produce cheap energy that, in many economic operations, could replace human muscle, reduce the time necessary to do things, and increase productivity and lower costs for many popular goods.

The Industrial Revolution reduced the prices of many broadly necessary goods, making them more available at low prices to many. In the process, it also destroyed the jobs of many previously self-employed workers, creating unemployment for many individuals. At times this would lead to violent reactions by the losers, some directed toward the machines.

The Industrial Revolution and the more democratic institutions, in time, would open the possibility, for governments, to increase tax levels, in order to begin to meet the growing demands for higher social spending (such as for education) that were coming from the increasingly urban and more democratic populations. By that time several developments had taken or were taking place. They would lead to the policy changes that would come, in most countries, and especially in welfare states, mainly after the Second World War.

The closing decades of the nineteenth century would witness major developments, of which the following deserve specific mention.

First, there were the "Bismarck's pension reforms," the reforms that had been introduced in Germany by Chancellor Bismarck a few years after the German unification and at a time when Germany was enjoying great world prestige and growing power. The reforms were in part introduced to counter the growing attraction that socialism was having on German workers. The socialist party had become a major political force in Germany and had started to challenge the existing political establishment.

The Bismarck reforms were also introduced to respond to the growing workers' pressure for better working conditions in the enterprises where they worked and at a time when some of those enterprises had become huge, remained largely untaxed, and were unregulated monopolies earning huge profits. These enterprises held much of the economic power vis-à-vis the workers who worked in them and who had no or little economic alternatives. In his writings, starting as early as 1948, Karl Marx had been stressing this aspect.

In those years a cooperative movement was also growing in importance, in part inspired by some altruistic employers, especially in the Catholic part of Germany and in parts of the north of Italy and in Austria. This movement was making it easier for some banks to extend loans to small enterprises, including some in the agricultural sector; and for some workers to organize, to better promote their economic interests (see Tanzi, 2011).

Some related developments were going on in the United States and in other countries. In the United States, the period that followed the Civil War would be an extraordinary period of growth which would witness the rise of "big business," as described by Porter (1992) and the Gilded Age period, when a new, small, rich, and privileged class, with enormous economic wealth and a great faith in its ability to change the world, had come into existence.

The members of this new class were increasingly feeling different from the rest of the population, as very rich people often do. They felt that they were fully entitled to their privileged positions and wealth. Some of them had even started marrying titled, but less rich, European nobles, to accentuate their class difference and to stress their similarity to the old European aristocracies. They were also rich enough to easily corrupt local public administrators, as had been happening in New York and other places.

At this time the United States had started to consider itself ready to take a leading role in world affairs, by abandoning its past isolationism. Its labor scarcity and its abundance of good land and natural resources had been attracting millions of workers from Europe and Asia, thus rapidly increasing its population. Many of these immigrants were escaping poverty or persecution and discrimination in the places where they came from. They were more likely to see the United States and its higher wages as a land of freedom and opportunity, in spite of some problems and occasional discrimination that some of them would experience in those and later years.

It was also a period when enormous public works, some of which seemed to challenge the limits of what had seemed technologically feasible in the past, were being undertaken, including the opening of the Panama Canal, the building of the Brooklyn Bridge, the completion of the transcontinental railroads networks, the creation of the telegraph system, the electrification of cities, the irrigation of desert areas of California, using water that came from hundreds of miles away, allowing enormous cities – such as Los Angeles and Phoenix – to be created in areas that had been deserts.

At the beginning of the new century, President Theodor Roosevelt had been determined to make the United States a major, or even the major, world power, as it had become, or was becoming, the major industrial power. Its foreign policies would be affected and would start to change.

In this period, names such as Vanderbilt, Carnegie, Rockefeller, Morgan, Du Pont, and others became synonymous with enormous wealth and economic power. For sure, they were not examples of actors operating in a "perfect, competitive market," the one implied by some pro-market economists. Rather, they were actors that felt that they had the power, the vision, and the means to change the world and to establish their own rules in that world. The distribution of income or equity were not their concern, only the rise of total output and of their wealth. However, it should be added that some of them left a large part of their wealth to foundations, universities, and churches that benefited society, such as Carnegie, Rockefeller, and others.

In the United States the cooperative movement did not develop, as it had in some parts of Europe, and socialism became less of an attraction among American workers, who continued to be more interested in higher wages and better working conditions, for them and for their families, than in changing the political structure of the country. Few American workers would join the communist party and not many joined the socialist movement.

As a conservative author would put it: "Before [1913] the macroeconomic performance of the United States, by the main measurements [i.e., GDP and industrial growth], was regular and strong," and "the most impressive half century in American ... economic history was that that followed the Civil War, the nearly 50 years from 1865 to 1913" (Domitrovic, 2010, p. 4).

This was the period when the American West was won and the United Stated became a continental country, one that stretched from the Atlantic to the Pacific. Domitrovic, as many other authors, showed no interest in how that output was being distributed among the population in those years. The focus was economic growth.

Second, there were the writings of a few leading economists who had become somewhat less enamored with the prevailing laissez faire ideology, an ideology that increasingly seemed to favor the *haves* over the *have nots*, and that had remained largely silent about the growing and glaring income and wealth inequality that had developed in those years. Henry George's book, *Progress and Poverty* (1879), would attract a lot of attention, and so would Veblen's (1899) work that criticized the "conspicuous consumption" by the new rich.

In 1848, Karl Marx had already been writing articles about the poor conditions of workers in modern factories who had no power over their working conditions (see Marx and Engels, 1848). By the late nineteenth century some leading photographers had started directing their work toward the conditions of the poor in places such as New York.

Especially important, or perhaps more globally and academically important in those years, would be the writings of Adolf Wagner, a leading German economist, who argued that the economic growth and the industrial development, then taking place at a fast rate, were bound to be accompanied by, or to lead to, the growth of the activities of the state. This view came to be called "Wagner's Law." It was a "law" that the true believers in laissez faire would challenge, but some economists and other experts would accept. Wagner also argued that some redistribution of income and of wealth would become inevitable and desirable, to maintain social peace.

Wagner's work, that went against the laissez faire dogma, attracted a lot of attention and large followings, both in Germany and in other countries. It contributed to changing some minds, even among previously mainstream economists. Many years later, the American economist William Baumol would support the view of the unavoidable rise in the share of public spending in GDP, but he would attribute this growth to the different impact of productivity gains in private and public activities. Lower productivity gains in some of the activities financed by the public sector, such as education, the arts, defense, and some others, would lead to growing relative costs of those activities and to an increasing share of public spending into GDP.

Third, there was the important and economically focused Encyclical Letter, *the Rerum Novarum*, that Pope Leon XIII published in 1891 on the conditions of labor. The letter described the poor economic conditions of the industrial workers at that time and called for better conditions and for "just wages" for them. It directly challenged the prevailing laissez faire ideology, at a time when the European bourgeoisie was showing, with great pride, its great technological achievements and the modern marvels that the Industrial Revolution had been producing, with "The Universal Exposition" in Paris and with that newly built architectural marvel, made of steel, the Eiffel Tower, The Eiffel Tower had been built to commemorate the first 100-year anniversary of the French Revolution. At that time, it was the tallest man-made structure on earth.

At the same time, in 1892 there would be the enormous 400 years celebration, in Chicago, of Columbus "discovery" of America, that would attract millions of visitors to Chicago.

Those were also the years when the colossal project that would be the Transcontinental Railroad in the United States was being completed (see Ambrose, 2000) and the work on the other colossal project, the opening of the Panama Canal, was being planned, by the same French engineer who had successfully opened the Suez Canal a couple of decades earlier. The French-financed Panama project would fail, because of major natural and financial difficulties encountered, and because of serious, tropical, infectious diseases among the workers who were working on the project. A few years later, a United States financed project, sponsored by President T. Roosevelt, and using a different design, would succeed. For the first time the Panama Canal would provide easy access to ships to navigate from the Atlantic Ocean to the Pacific Ocean, at a time when global trade was growing at a fast pace.

The Pope's *Encyclical Letter* addressed two of the main social questions of the day: the legitimate right to private property, which had been questioned by socialists, and the workers' right to a just wage and to free association. These had become much discussed topics at that time. The *Letter* flatly rejected the claims that socialism, which would eliminate private property, could be a desirable alternative ideology for a free society. However, while the Encyclical Letter defended the right to private property, and the need for differences in income and wealth among individuals (justifying them on grounds of natural differences in innate talent, in abilities, and in efforts), it called for more economic "justice," for more "charity," and for more intervention by the state in social questions. This definition of justice contrasted with the socialists "economic justice" for whom justice simply meant income equality and the abolition of private property.

The *Encyclical Letter* stressed that there were personal interests as well as community, or social, interests that were equally important. In some ways, the *Encyclical Letter* could be read as a rejection not only of socialism but also of the extreme form of laissez faire, and as an early acceptance of some form of welfare state.

Half a century later, in 1951, Kenneth Arrow would deal with somewhat similar issues, from a theoretical point of view, in his book. *Social Choice and Individual Values.* He would stress the need to recognize social or community choices, but also the difficulties of doing so, in a market economy based on individual choices. Those difficulties have not disappeared since that time. In 1971, in a book that would attract a lot of attention and interest, John Rawls, a leading philosopher, would discuss similar issues to those that had been dealt by the Pope's *Encyclical Letter* a century earlier.

Fourth, from March 15 to March 28, 1890, there would be, in Berlin, the first "World Conference on the Protection of Workers." This conference would propose May 1 as *Labor Day*, the day to officially celebrate workers. That day had been chosen to remember a tragic episode that had taken place in May 1886 in a US factory in Chicago, when several striking workers had been shot and killed during an unauthorized workers' strike. The event came to be called the Haymarket Riot. Some anarchists, who had taken part in the strike, were later convicted, and some were executed after quick trials.

In the United States a Labor Day celebration would be introduced in later years, by President Cleveland. It would fall on the first Monday of

September. The Berlin World Conference also strongly pushed for the right of workers to unionize, and for limiting the working day to 8 hours, instead of the then 12 hours.

Clearly the last decade of the nineteenth century was one of great changes, not only in terms of technological achievements, but especially in social attitudes. It was showing increasing concern for the way societies were organized and the way the gains from the Industrial Revolution were being shared. The old world was starting to give more space to a new world, in Europe earlier than in the United States.

The beginning of the new century would bring further changes, and the changes would give increasing importance to equity, and to the role that the government could play in the economy. In the United States, the new attitude would bring the regulation of monopolies, by President T. Roosevelt; the introduction of a permanent income tax in 1913, which required an amendment to the US Constitution; and the creation of the Federal Reserve System, that would bring a national currency and create the possibility for the national government to use monetary policy and credit obtained from the central bank. All these changes would continue to be opposed by the true believers in laissez faire and would be introduced after hard political battles.

For these reasons the beginning of the twentieth century would be called the "Progressive Age," an age when it became more acceptable to begin to reduce some of the excessive power of the superrich and of the monopolies that they had created and to pay more attention to the welfare of the masses (see Diner, 1998).

7

Toward Larger Government Roles

Some fundamental changes in the role of government would have to wait until the Great Depression in the 1930s, and even the end of the Second World War, which would bring the New Deal in the United States and welfare reforms in the United Kingdom and other countries. Before that happened, there would be the "roaring twenties," a period when there would be a first attempt to go back to laissez faire policies in the United States.

A second attempt would come in the late 1970s and the 1980s with the Thatcher and Reagan reforms in the United Kingdom and the United States, respectively. In Russia and some other countries, the twentieth century would bring the first real-life experiment with Marxist socialism and central planning. These experiments would represent the total abandonment of the capitalist system of running economies and give us an indication of the consequences of doing so. In countries which had retained market economies, economists in governments realized that there were "failures" in the way the free market had been working, and in the 1930s there would be the beginning of attempts at correcting those failures. However, strong intellectual and class-based resistance to the corrections would continue to come from both conservative economists and others.

Many economists and others continued to have faith in the efficiency of the market and little faith in the ability of governments to bring changes that might have seemed necessary, at least on equity grounds. Some economists continued to assume that, whatever shortcomings the capitalist system might have, they were minor and transitory, and that the market was capable of correcting itself over the long-term, while maintaining individual freedom that, in principle, made it possible for anyone to succeed. Furthermore, the shortcomings and the costs to economies created by worker requests, or by government interventions, might be major, and might create long-term difficulties. The pursuit of equity continued to be seen as an obstacle to efficiency, and efficiency continued to be given importance.

Typical of this thinking were the views of Wilhelm Ropke, a famous German economist who had left Germany during Hitler's time and who lived and taught in Switzerland. Those views, originally expressed in a newspaper article in 1958, may be worth citing:

> ... once we accept the principle of compulsion, which is inseparable from the welfare state even in the case of social security, as a means of assisting the individual in his struggle against the vicissitude of life – where, then, is the limit? Might we not find that things get out of hand, as happened with progressive taxation ... It would be hard to deny that the welfare state progresses by its own momentum and, in striking analogy with progressive taxation, there is nothing in its conception to set a limit to it".
>
> (Ropke, 1969, p. 204)

He compared the welfare state to "a powerful machine that has neither breaks nor reverse gears" and believed that "in a democracy we are likely to get too much welfare state rather than too little." He cited the Scandinavian countries as countries in which the welfare state had already gone too far. These were typical libertarian views after the Second World War. Similar views had been expressed by von Mises.

Before the United States entered the First World War, American workers had been doing better, during the "Progressive Era." The war had required a great increase in manufacturing to produce armaments and satisfy Europe's large demand for military and other goods. Wages and employment had gone up and had stayed up during the war period. Conditions for workers had also improved. The new century had seen some decline in both faith in laissez faire and in the practice of its extreme form.

However, when the war ended, production fell and so did the demand for labor. At about the same time, the Bolshevik Revolution in Russia was in full swing. Employers tried to reduce real wages and to restore some of the controls on workers' actions that had been lacking in the laissez faire environment in the past and that had survived to some extent in the memory of many employers during the Progressive Age.

Thousands of strikes followed, after the war, and many of them turned violent. There had never been so many strikes in the US economy as there were in 1919, when four million workers went on strike over cuts in wages and over attempts by employers to worsen their working conditions. These developments attracted a lot of attention in the media, and interest from some intellectuals.

Many politicians and employers became convinced that the strikes in the United States were partly coordinated by socialists and were related to, and inspired by, what was happening in Russia. Resistance to the strikes intensified. Strikes in Seattle and Boston were particularly violent, as was a national strike in several steel mills in different cities that had been coordinated by labor unions and that had reduced the national production of steel by 60 percent.

The strikers were often confronted by thugs hired by their employers. Accusation of communist influences and fears of a Russian-style revolution in the United States intensified, leading to even more drastic reactions by employers, which in turn resulted in more strikes and some workers' deaths. A major pandemic (the Spanish Flu) contributed to the chaos and the sense of doom.

At that time there were also some race riots against the Black population, in Chicago and especially in Tulsa, Oklahoma, where hundreds of Black people were killed. There were also widespread lynchings, especially in the South. Bombs were placed by anarchists in several places. This was also the period when "eugenic" theories, of the presumed superiority of some races or some ethnic groups over others, had become popular in some quarters. They would lead to sharp cuts in immigration from Eastern and Southern Europe, and to the expansion of the activities of the Ku Klux Klan, as reflected in the book, *The Guarded Gate*, by Okrent (2019), and the old movie "The Birth of a Nation." It has been reported that these views may have had some influence on Hitler's own racial views and on the rise of Nazism in Germany. Many presumed "Reds," or "communists," were arrested and, if they happened to be foreign born, they were quickly deported. This signaled the end of the "Progressive Era," and the United States turned very conservative for the next decade, until the 1930s.

Some related developments would lead to the advent of Fascism in Italy and, later, of Nazism in Germany, and there would be a bloody civil war in Spain. Some of these European developments may have been the consequence of the Treaty of Versailles, that accompanied the end of the First World War. That treaty had been sharply criticized by Keynes, who had been present during the discussions in Versailles, and had seen the impossibility of Germany respecting the Treaty (see Keynes, 1920).

By the 1920s the US economy and society had in part returned closer to the pre-Progressive Age. They had become economically more conservative with much less immigration. The feared "Red" revolution had not happened but continued to be feared, and the "business" of America had returned to mainly "business," with conservative administrations for a decade and with a lot of speculation in the, little regulated, stock market.

The decade would come to be known as the "roaring twenties," typified by consumerism and economic freedom, until the advent of that other tragic event "the Great Depression," which would start with the stock market collapse of October 1929, created by too much lending and speculation. The Great Depression would decimate US economic output and employment and lead to the election of F. D. Roosevelt, and to the "New Deal," beginning a new era lasting several decades.

In the 1920s unrestrained laissez faire and much optimism had returned to guide the American economy, accompanied by highly conservative policies, policies that had become a little less conservative in the years before the First World War. The Depression would bring some new economic thinking, including the Keynesian Revolution, which would dominate until the 1970s, and the policies of the New Deal. The next attempt to return to laissez faire policies would come in the late 1970s.

The limited and partial abandonment of the laissez faire ideology during the Great Depression became, for some conservative economists, an explanation for the events that led to it. Many continued to believe that, if wages and prices had remained flexible enough, if free trade had been maintained, and if monetary policies had been adequate, there would not have been a *Great* Depression. They would mention that, in the past, when there had been wage flexibility and freedom to fire workers, there had been occasional deep depressions, but they had lasted for brief periods, without the intervention of government. In their view the Great Depression of the 1930s became *great* and different because of the interference by the government in the free market. See Solimano (2020) for an account of past depressions, some rather deep, but shorter.

There has continued to be a natural and strong opposition to changes in the dogma of the free market and a belief in the virtue of the laissez faire system among conservative economists, convinced capitalists, and many of those, especially richer individuals, who feel that they would personally lose from policy changes, as some rich people had when income taxes and controls over monopolies were introduced.

Laissez faire had been considered a *stable* system, one in which many implicit rules and the behavior of market participants would not change in spite of the likely increase in the number and power of rich individuals. These rich individuals are likely to develop common interests and to join forces to promote their interests.

Adam Smith's warning about market abuses was generally ignored. His warning had been that, when market operators have the opportunity, they are likely to create "cartels" and to engage in other schemes, to increase their profits.

What was true in Smith's time is likely to be even truer today, when associations and contacts among rich people are far easier and when they can influence the media with their money (see also Solimano, 2014). A concentration of wealthy individuals in various types of elite networks is likely to create such opportunities, as we shall discuss in more detail in later chapters.

For less conservative economists, whose number had increased over the years, the greater are market failures, including failures in equity, employment, or allocation, the greater government intervention in the market needs to be, especially when the failures lead to low growth or income distribution that becomes progressively more uneven. This was in part the justification for the creation of welfare states. This should happen unless there is a belief or expectation that the market failures would be inevitably followed by "government failures," and that the latter would be greater than the market failures.

This view formed a major part of the School of Public Choice, the school of thought that James Buchanan and others created in the 1960s, and that in the years that followed became increasingly popular in academia, and not just in the United States (see Mueller, 1989). Some writers have seen a darker side, or even a "stealth plan" or a conspiracy, in the creation of that school, which was reported to have been partly financed by conservative, wealthy individuals (see MacLean, 2017).

The government intervention that in 1919–1920 many Americans had feared the most was a Marxist-style intervention, one that would eliminate property rights and individual freedom and would introduce central planning, replacing the market. This had been the plan of socialist forces and leaders including Karl Marx. Hayek wrote about this type of intervention in his best-selling and influential book, *The Road to Serfdom*, published in 1944. That book was abridged and published by both the Readers' Digest and The Heritage Foundation. It was translated into ten languages and sold millions of copies. That book would define Hayek, then already a famous economist, not only as a scholar but as a "prophet," and

reduce the interest of economists in his later works which gave some scope
to a government role in a free market.

Some of Hayek's limited new views or actions might have been controversial for some economists, including his flirtation with authoritarian
leaders such as Salazar in Portugal and Pinochet in Chile, or his proposal
to denationalize money which seemed to anticipate current interest in bit
coin and cryptocurrency. But these do not reduce the value of his
major work.

Roles of government that were softer and less radical, and that would
later be introduced in several countries that were still capitalist, were
resisted by those who continued to embrace principles of free markets
and libertarian policies and who saw deviations from those policies as
"roads to serfdom." At the same time more economists had started to
consider the possibility and the realism of "middle ground" or "third
ways" policies (see Giddens, 1998). However, many conservative economists continued to label almost any governmental intervention as a
"socialist policy." See, for example, Ropke (1969) and the papers in
Woods Jr (2010).

As mentioned, Hayek's later writings, especially those published a
couple of decades later, though they remained strongly pro-market, had
started to recognize some governmental interventions in the economy as
necessary. By that time, he must not have seen all government interventions as necessarily leading to "serfdom." See Machlup (1976b,
pp. 13–51) and Tanzi (2015).

This change must have made him less than a full member of the
Chicago School, and in particular his view that: "[n]obody can be a great
economist if he is only an economist . . . and an economist who is only an
economist is likely to become a nuisance if not a positive danger" must
not have ingratiated him in a place (the University of Chicago) where his
colleagues firmly believed in the "religious" truth of economic theory.

The impression that one gets is that, in spite of his strong libertarian
and pro-market views, Hayek never became an integral part of the
Chicago School of Economics. He lacked the sharp edges that characterized his colleagues. He left Chicago and spent the rest of his life in Europe.

Starting in the 1930s, an increasing number of observers and economists had started to see the government as a possible and even a necessary
input in an economy and in a society, and as a possible complement to the
"good" work of the market, but not as a replacement for it. Some started
to believe that market and government could coexist peacefully. For
reasons that were becoming more evident with the passing of time they

also believed that no market could operate well without *some* government role. However, intervention by the government should remain limited and well-focused, allowing the market to continue to perform much of its role in allocating resources and in generating income. The role of the government would remain a marginal and complementary one. When that role became large, it would lead to difficulties.

The questions that remained unanswered at that time, and that have remained controversial until now, are: What should the government role be? How large should it be? Should it correct mainly for failures in *allocation* of resources, or also for presumed "failures" in income *distribution*? And with what tools should that role be promoted?

These fundamental questions have received less attention than they should, perhaps in part because the opposing camps had continued to push for corner solutions, rejecting feasible or potential middle ground or "third ways." In the "third way" approach, while the government would bring the needed corrections, it should be prevented from becoming a substitute for the market, and its role would remain as limited as is realistically possible in the modern democratic world. How possible is that? This is the question that should have been addressed in depth but often was not and it has continued to be addressed only ideologically.

The government's intervention, of course, would depend on how distorted the market was seen to have become, and how efficient the government was expected to be to play its needed, corrective role, considering the pressures that would come from lobbies, political forces, and bureaucratic corruption. Other considerations include limitations that might be imposed by constitutions written centuries ago that are difficult to amend and that, at times, leave scope for interpretation by Supreme Court Judges who may have their own biases, as has been happening in the United States. This implies that the desired role of the government might have to be smaller in some countries than in others. Some scholars have remarked that the US Constitution makes no reference to *social* rights, only to *individual* rights.

The government role should include the important objective of promoting a minimum, expected income equity in a community that is not made up of isolated, individualistic operators who care mainly about themselves, but of individuals who have, or should have, some "empathy" for other members of the community, as Adam Smith recognized three centuries ago.

Individuals generally do not live in the isolation of a Robinson Crusoe world, but in communities. One of government's roles should be to strengthen community spirit in various ways and not fight and weaken it, as excessive emphasis on individualism tends to do.

Until the Great Depression, the prevalent view had been that, in terms of resource allocation, market failures were relatively limited, easily identifiable, and correctable. They had to do with clear externalities, as had been stressed by the work of Pigou, in 1920, and with monopolies, monopsonies, and similar distortions. In later years, monopolistic competition, a market failure that could be more widespread and less easily recognizable than traditional monopolies, and that could take various forms, was added to the list, by Joan Robinson, in the United Kingdom, and by E. H. Chamberlin, in the United States.

In the 1950s economists realized that the market failures might be more numerous and that some might exist even in what might seem to be "efficient markets" (see Bator, 1958). In this context, "public goods" came to be seen as especially important.

Although the existence of public goods had been known for a long time, especially in the Italian literature – by Mazzola, De Viti De Marco, and others – the precise identifications of their characteristics became clear only in the mid-1950s, after Paul Samuelson published his two important articles, in 1954 and 1955. See Head (1974) and Cornes and Sandler (1986) for discussions.

Quasi-public goods, which are public goods with one but not both of the qualities of pure public goods identified by Samuelson (joint consumption and free riding) attracted increasing attention in the late 1950s and in later years. Some of them were seen as important in creating equal opportunities for citizens in the welfare systems that were being created in those years.

Until the 1930s, relatively few mainstream economists (as opposed to workers, who had been less concerned with the *general* distribution of income and more with the value of their real wages) had considered an uneven income distribution and a high unemployment rate as examples of *market* failures that could be corrected by governmental intervention. However, some economists, and workers with socialist or leftist tendencies, had seen unemployment and an uneven income distribution or low real wages as undesirable features of a capitalist society, which a socialist economy promised to eliminate. Some of them would point out that centrally planned, socialist economies did not have open unemployment.

Many, but still far from all economists, now consider an income distribution that has become significantly uneven, as it has in recent decades in several countries, as a particular kind of market or, at least, social failure, unless the very high incomes received by some individuals have clearly originated from exceptional and legitimate contributions to output, and the low incomes of others are caused by their refusal to accept offered market wages. After the Great Depression, Keynesian economists came to consider high unemployment as a clear market failure, one that could be corrected with adequate macro policies.

However, the view that continued to prevail among many conservative economists continued to be that, in the absence of monopolies and other abuses, people receive incomes that broadly reflect what they (or, in the case of income from inherited wealth, their ancestors) contribute to national production, with their labor, their effort, and their savings. Therefore, the incomes that the market determines for them must be considered genuine *incomes*. *They* should not be considered, wholly or partly, *rents*, that is, earnings that are not truly "earned" or "merited."

Whether incomes should be subjected to progressive taxes or not, and how progressive the taxes ought to be, is a separate issue, and the answer may in part depend on how uneven the income distribution has become, on the community spirit that exists in the country, and on how the revenues collected are spent. The more even the income distribution, the less strong the case for progressive taxation becomes.

Views on the importance of equity had started to change slowly about a century ago, and the change intensified in the 1930s, during the Depression, and after the Second World War, when the unevenness in the distribution of income and the impact it had on the standards of living of individuals and families came to be seen, at least by some, as the result of abuses of the market, abuses created by manipulated laws and regulations, or by corrupt practices by market participants, or even by excess savings by richer people combined with a low propensity to invest. Corruption, rent seeking, and other practices, however, have attracted increasing attention only since the 1990s, whereas deficient aggregate demand had attracted attention in the 1930s.

In more recent years, there has been some realization that the implicit or formal rules that guide markets and the behavior of market participants are never completely neutral and stable. They are inevitably influenced by the distribution of the political power that existed when the rules were first introduced, and by the changes in the interpretation of those rules that have reflected the changes in power over the years. This is true even for laissez faire rules, which ignore the role of inherited wealth. The rules keep changing all the time, in visible and often in less visible ways, and they change in ways that are more favorable to those who are more able to influence them, who are usually the wealthier individuals. And there cannot be a society without some rules.

The free market and laissez faire policies have continued to attract followers, as indicated by the many "think tanks" that exist in the United States, United Kingdom, Canada, Australia, Italy, and other countries, and that continue to promote the view of an ideal free market, a market that creates opportunities and freedom for all.

Such a market never existed or could have existed, except when individuals depended solely on their personal hunting. The market's "true believers" believe that a fair and free market, one completely free of influences and one that can genuinely contribute more to output, can exist, without the intervention of the government. In the rest of this book, we shall argue that this view is naïve and that things are much more complex in the real world.

This chapter will be concluded by citing directly the way a sophisticated, libertarian expert has recently described the free market. The views were reported in a blog dated May 2022, published by a respected British, libertarian "think tank" (Politeia). The blog was written by a prominent and presumably knowledgeable, conservative individual (Anthony Coombs, Chair of the finance company S&U and a former Member of Parliament (MP)). It is reported here not because it is extreme in the views expressed but because it represents a typical description of a common way of thinking among libertarian and conservative individuals.

The blog starts by stating that "the bedrock conservatism has always been in trusting the people, in particular the notion that the efforts of individuals to better themselves and their families within a minimally regulated economy and system of law that encourages entrepreneurship, will generally be more effective in raising standards for every citizen …" It continues: "A rising tide will lift all boats," and "Without that freely rising tide … the leveling up simply becomes a process of bureaucratic confiscation [from the more productive wealthy to the less productive poor]." Mr. Coombs never describes "the minimally regulated economy and the system of law that would encourage intrapreneurship." One is left to imagine what that minimally regulated economy would be.

Mr. Coombs complains about the "deadweight of excessive taxation" and about the common assumption that profit often implies exploitation. He complains about the monitoring of "consumer detriment" by regulators, implying that there are no such abuses, in spite of the daily news reports on such abuses (see, for example, Knowles, 2022). He complains about the role that civil servants and politicians play in the "leveling up process," which he claims they do inefficiently, which, of course, is in part true. Should the focus be on making that process more efficient, rather than just criticizing it?

In conclusion, the message that Mr. Coombs gives to the British government is to get out of the way and let the free market and the leveling down process (through "trickle down") and the leveling up (through "more effort by the individuals") do their work. Accept any distributional results that the market generates as fair, and do not tax them, or tax them only lightly. The implicit message seems to be: Let us get back to the 1920s; or let us get back to the laissez faire of the nineteenth century, and we shall *all, rich and poor*, live happily.

PART II

FROM LAISSEZ FAIRE TO WELFARE STATES:
1930 TO 1970

8

The Growing Importance of Equity and Safety Nets

After the Second World War and the tragic experience of the Great Depression, the number of economists and average citizens who continued to believe that the government should play no role in redistributing income, in creating some essential safety nets for citizens and families, and in promoting economic stability fell. The pursuit of more equity with full employment rose in importance in government policies. Of course, there remained strong political opposition to the change and doubts and disagreements on how well the government could perform these new functions and how much redistribution it could attempt to promote with its policies without damaging the traditional role of the market.

Some economists continued to believe that the best policy would still be one of free markets, flexible wages, and very limited government intervention, policies that presumably "would create trickle down and lift all boats" over the long-term. Support for the role of the government in promoting equity, by limiting abuses and through some active social policies and not just by correcting presumed or theoretical allocative inefficiencies, increased in those years. However, it never ceased to be controversial for conservative economists and citizens.

Pro-market economists, such as Robert Lucas, who would become an important Nobel Prize Laureate, argued that the government should play no role in making the distribution of income more equal. In his strongly held view, such a role would distort the market allocation of resources and reduce the market efficiency and the freedom of individuals. In Lucas' view the market made few or no mistakes and was efficient and equitable. Other conservative economists and politicians shared Lucas' view. For example, a colleague of Lucas at "The Chicago School," who, at that time, was a very visible and influential economist, stated that concern for inequality was due in part to "a naive and basically infantile anthropomorphism" (Johnson, 1973, p. 54).

On the other hand, many economists, including Amartya Sen, also an important Nobel Laureate, argued that more equality in results, or, at least, more equality in providing similar opportunities or similar starting conditions, to all citizens, must be a fundamental governmental responsibility, because individuals are not born with equal opportunities. When that is the case, the belief that a free market will make *all* people equally free and will provide them with equal opportunity for economic success is a cruel illusion.

Poverty can be seen as a limitation of liberty, even in free democratic countries, as Sen stressed. Many economists and plain citizens share Sen's view, a view that has received considerable academic and political backing in recent years. Some economists have argued that we do not live in a world where the allocation of resources is optimal but in a world of "second best," and "second best" is not the same as "optimal."

John Rawls (1971), a philosophy professor at Harvard, published a book called *A Theory of Justice*. In 1993 he followed that book with a second book, *Political Liberalism*. Both books attracted a lot of attention and were discussed for many years. Both dealt with distributive justice, the same justice that the Pope had dealt with in his 1891 Encyclical Letter.

Rawls proposed two basic principles of Justice. The first stated that each person is entitled to a fully adequate scheme of equal *basic* rights and liberties (essentially equal political liberties). These rights should be guaranteed by the state and be enshrined in political constitutions. The second principle stated that social and economic inequalities, when they exist, must satisfy two conditions: the first is that they must accompany positions or offices to which *all* individuals can accede, under similar opportunity. Therefore, birth rights would play no role in obtaining these positions, as they had often played in the past. The second condition is that the inequalities that exist must benefit the least advantaged the most.

The second condition has been known as the "Difference Principle." In Rawls thinking, political liberties cannot be sacrificed in order to provide better material standards of living, even to the least advantaged. Therefore, the Marxist alternative is not legitimate. However, some differences in incomes *can* be justified if those differences especially help those at the bottom, that is if there is genuine evidence that they will increase output and significantly generate "trickle down."

Rawls principle is useful in directing us to the basic questions to address, in justifying inequality that exists: how much inequality should be tolerated in a democratic country with a market economy? The evidence that we have from the past four decades indicates that this question has not been addressed. Clearly, Rawls principle cannot be used to justify the inequality that was created in the United States, the United Kingdom, and some other countries in the decades after the 1970s.

The Rawls principle can be interpreted to imply that if higher incomes for some individuals lead to more productivity by them, and if that higher productivity helps the poorest by creating good and well-paying jobs for them, then inequality may be justified. It rules out equal income as a principle of justice, because it is likely to conflict with the basic civil rights, or with efficient economic behavior. It also rules out a situation where many of the jobs created are low, minimum wages jobs.

The Rawls principle obviously depends on the assumption that higher compensation for some people (Managers of enterprises? Financial operators? Others?) makes them significantly more productive but that they do not entirely appropriate all the growth in that productivity. It also raises the question as to how much income differences (how much higher compensations) are required to promote the desired productivity benefit. Is there a limit to these differences? If yes, how big is that limit?

These questions have remained highly controversial, as income differences have increased over the years, while productivity and the compensation of average workers have not, and questions have been increasingly raised as to whether these income differences have been affecting the equality of economic liberty, by the impact that they have had on the political power of rich elites.

Returning to Lucas and Sen, which of the alternatives, both sustained by equally important Nobel Prize Winners in Economics, is more legitimate would seem to depend on how well the market truly performs, both its allocative and its distributional role, and how much importance society attributes to luck, to initial conditions (such as what has been called "the birth lottery"), and to other market manipulations in determining economic results (see Chetty et al., 2014). The better the market performs, and the more society focuses on the individual rather than the community, the more weight Lucas' view acquires, at least with economists. The less well the market performs, and the more importance is assigned to community values, the more legitimacy Sen's position would seem to have.

Daily reports in the news seem to indicate that abuses and other problems have continued and probably have even increased with the use of the Internet and the liberalization of the financial market. What do they tell us about the operation of the market? Are all the problems, including internet scams and financial abuses caused by the existence of government rules, as some libertarians continue to believe? If there were no rules, would these abuses magically disappear? If we abolish the concept of sin or of crimes, there would no longer be sinners or criminals? One is entitled to doubt the wisdom of these options.

At times, the market might be efficient and equitable enough to require, or to justify, little or no government's intervention, or little needed change in the actual policies. Exceptionally talented individuals, even when they come from very low social and economic backgrounds, or are immigrants, as many are, occasionally do well in markets that retain some flexibility. They do particularly well in sport activity. Even Pope Leon XIII had recognized that a free market could not provide *equal* incomes to all, because not all individuals have the same capacity and the same ability to work and produce, even when circumstances are made broadly similar.

Some inequality is clearly necessary to promote efficiency and even for equity reasons and some income differences are necessary to retain the necessary incentives for individuals. The questions that remain unanswered are: how much inequality is needed to sustain the efficiency of the market? Is it possible that too much inequality may set in motion forces that in the long-term reduce the efficiency of an economy by promoting popular support for bad policies and/or by transferring too much income to "rents"? Or by leading to the creation of elites that have the power to influence policies and the interpretation of laws and regulations, to promote their self-interest? These are important questions that ought not be ignored.

In any case, especially in a modern democratic society, too much inequality is likely to be resented, and is especially resented when there are also doubts about the efficiency and the fairness of the market. Daily news or daily evidence about abuses by some superrich do not help. Neither do reports about some of their spending habits.

There may be times when the market might require more intervention, either to improve resource allocation or to make outcomes more equitable, and the intervention must be the desired one, in terms of equity and efficiency. It can be argued that there should be some harmony between what citizens (and economists) expect from the market and what the market is delivering. But these expectations should be based on reality and not just on theories or perceptions.

A question that should always be asked is: how much is the existing inequality contributing to making the economy more efficient and the citizens freer? And how much is it helping the common citizens, especially the poorest citizens? How well would the government be able to perform acts of correction? How could it generate more harmony with its actions and its policies? Can its interventions make the situation worse? Should the growth of GDP or the employment rate be the only or the main criteria for judging the performance of the market, as it has often been for economists? Or should the statistics be better analyzed in terms of their utilitarian impact and their impact on all workers and citizens? Has each dollar of GDP generated have the same value in terms of general welfare?

According to available surveys, this harmony seems to have been approximated, even if never precisely achieved, in the United States only occasionally and for brief periods. Perhaps some such harmony was achieved, briefly, in the mid-1960s and, again, in the mid-1990s. When the right balance or the harmony is seen to be significantly broken, as it has been, for different reasons especially in some periods, the role of the government or the operation of the market, or both, should change. Unfortunately, the needed changes often come late and, when they come, they may not be sufficient or may occasionally go too far or be the wrong changes. This, in turn, will create new future difficulties.

This happened several times in the past, when major disequilibria were created, between the actual role of the state and its expected, normative role. This may have happened in the 1920s. In some cases, the role *of the market* was excessively reduced. This may have happened in the late 1960s and 1970s, because of the excessive power of the labor unions and the very high marginal tax rates in those years. In 1964, the Pew Research Center reported that, in the United States, trust in government had been as high as 77 percent, a record. It would sharply fall a few years later.

This also happened when the market was expected to perform miracles and, in the process, the changes that were made excessively *reduced the role of the government*. This may have happened in the 1980s and 1990s, with the advent of very conservative policymakers and policies, in icountries such as the United States, the United Kingdom, and some others, and with their promotion of "market fundamentalist" policies that corrected some earlier mistakes in resource allocation but went too far.

The changes that started taking place after the introduction of the new conservative policies, in the late 1970s and 1980s onwards, may have corrected some previous mistakes but, in time, they created others. They proved unable to generate the economic miracle that they had promised, the miracle that would "lift all boats." The new policies would lead to growing difficulties in future years.

Before leaving this chapter, it might be mentioned that the view that the state should somehow regulate the wealth distribution, at a time when, in the past, the emphasis was on wealth and not on income, had occasionally been mentioned by important thinkers of the distant past, such as Aristotle (see *Politics*, Book V, chapter 1) and Montesquieu, *Esprit des Lois*, Book V, chapter VI and others. Therefore, it was not a new view. In the recent world, to some extent and for various reasons, the emphasis has shifted from wealth to income distribution.

9

The Creation of Welfare States

By the end of the nineteenth century, the Industrial Revolution had advanced enough to be hiring many workers in industrial activities and to have radically transformed the economic environment that had existed in the past. The change had made the need for new policies and for a larger government role increasingly and widely felt, as had been recognized by Adolf Wagner and others. It had also highlighted the importance of the capitalist system in the new economy. Without the capitalist system, it is not likely that the Industrial Revolution would have taken place as it did, or as fast as it did. Countries that were not influenced by the spirit of Capitalism developed less rapidly.

By that time there would be the beginning of some social and economic reforms in several countries, but the more significant ones would come later, mainly in the 1930s, initially and modestly in the United States, with the New Deal pushed by the experience of the Great Depression and by F. D. Roosevelt. More deep reforms would come after the Second World War, starting in the United Kingdom, but spreading to other European countries. The policy changes would progressively aim at closing the wide gap that had developed between the role of the state that many *citizens desired* and the *actual* roles that governments had been pursuing.

The reforms would also bring some important changes in the private sector, first through new regulations of private activities and then through the impact of higher taxes, public spending, and the rise of powerful labor unions that would provide a counterweight to the power of the corporations. The world that had existed in the past was being increasingly challenged by the new developments and a new world was fast coming into existence. The new world would require new institutions, including a different and larger government role.

Adolf Wagner had recognized that need toward the end of the nineteenth century, and Keynes had also recognized the need for significant changes in the mid-1920s, in a small book appropriately called *The End of Laissez Faire* (Keynes, 1926). In that book, he had strongly stated his belief that the then existing world needed significant policy changes to continue to exist.

President F. D. Roosevelt would recognize this need, in the United States, a few years later, in the middle of the Great Depression, by introducing for the first time the then radical policies of the *New Deal*. The new policies included some social programs, such as Social Security pensions for retired people, higher tax rates for high incomes, and important regulations of some financial activities, in addition to major public works' programs that provided government jobs to many unemployed workers while providing some needed public goods. These policies would significantly expand the economic role of the government in the United States and would make the capitalist system more equitable (see Schlesinger, 1959; 1960). The new policies faced strong oppositions from conservative forces that remained opposed to the changes.

The Great Depression not only accelerated some of the changes that had been underway, it also raised fundamental questions and doubts, in the minds of an increasing number of economists and the general public, about the claimed virtue of the capitalist system, when that system was guided by the laissez faire ideology, as it had been until 1932. This was at a time when, in the United States, the unemployment rate had reached 25 percent of the labor force, and, in other countries, such as Australia, 30 percent; and when output had collapsed in many countries.

At that time there had been no safety nets to cushion the fall in the standards of living for those who lost their jobs, and for their families. Keynes would propose counter-cyclical, fiscal policies, that, if adopted, would contribute to the change in the future economic role of the government suggested by the "Keynesian Revolution." These policies were also strongly opposed by conservative individuals and by some leading economists, such as Hayek, who had continued to have faith in the free market. By the 1950s, the "Keynesian Revolution" had acquired many followers. For many of them it had become a new orthodoxy (see Klein, 1947).

After the Second World War, *redistribution* of income and *stabilization* of the economy had become new and integral parts of the governments' operations, in countries that were still guided by the capitalist system. The capitalist system had been "softened" a little, to make it cope with the wishes and the needs of the majority. These changes would bring the role of the government closer in line with the expectations of many people and, presumably, with what the market needed, although this remained a controversial issue with economists and politicians. The changes would help close the gap that had existed and had possibly widened in the decade of the 1920s between the desired and the actual roles of governments.

By the end of the Second World War:

a. Many advanced countries were facing more friendly *tax ecologies* that had made it easier for governments to raise taxes during the war and later. The tax environment had become considerably more friendly for governments because of the experience gained during the war in the administration of higher taxes (see Tanzi, 2018b).

b. Most citizens (including women) had acquired the right to vote, shifting the political weight toward lower income groups and toward higher social spending.

c. Advanced countries had become more urbanized, and cities had much higher needs for regulations and for some public goods than, in the past, had the agricultural and rural areas.

d. The attitudes of many, though by no means all, economists and plain citizens had changed and had become more welcoming to a larger and presumably more beneficial role that governments could play in promoting the welfare of most citizens and in stabilizing the economies. It should be added that, by that time, the government could hire more literate civil servants to administer its policies.

There were, of course, still many libertarian or conservative economists and politicians, as there are still today, that continued to believe in a world in which an economy could function smoothly and efficiently if guided by laissez faire principles and with incentives created by individual economic liberty, by limited regulations, and by low taxes. Especially in the United States, these economists continued to see higher taxes, even if collected to provide essential public goods, as exploitation by lazy citizens of those who worked and produced more.

Proposals for major changes in policies to be made after the war had been suggested in the United Kingdom, in 1942, in the politically influential Beveridge Report, a report which had become a bestseller during war time; and, in the United States, in a "fire chat" by President Roosevelt, delivered in 1944. Both had mentioned various peoples' needs that could be better met with the help of government policies and actions. Some of these policies would be introduced in the years after the war.

In 1950, the US Republican Party would still have enough popular support to win the election, with a popular general as its presidential candidate. Eisenhower's presidential acceptance speech made many references to the new role that the government would play in the US economy. This was significant, because he was representing the US conservative party. President Eisenhower would play an important role in building a national highway system in the United States financed by tax money. This was an important kind of "public good." His administration would be a relatively moderate one.

These are all indications of the ideological shift that had taken place by the 1940s, a shift that was being increasingly recognized, at least in part, even in conservative circles. Part of that shift had been the direct consequence of the Great Depression, an experience that had left deep scars in many American families. Another part of it was due to the War, and yet another part had been developing slowly, over longer periods.

The age of the "Keynesian Revolution" and that of the "welfare reforms," the reforms that would create welfare states in many countries, had arrived and would dominate the three decades that followed. Those reforms would be faster and deeper in many European countries than in the United States.

As already mentioned, by this time the structures of the economies had changed, making it easier for governments that wished to do so to collect higher tax revenue from broad-based taxes and to create the bureaucratic apparatus needed to implement and monitor the more complex government programs (see Fogel, 2000).

It could be argued that the normative and the positive roles of the government had started to converge in those years, at least in the perception of many economists and citizens. The harmony that should exist between the two roles had significantly increased and would become felt more by the mid-1960s, during the Kennedy years and President Johnsons' "War on Poverty" legislation. That legislation expanded the welfare measures introduced during the New Deal.

The feeling of harmony was clearly reflected in the important *Economic Reform of the President* of 1962, a report that had the contribution of three important future Nobel Prize Winners in

Economics – Samuelson, Solow, and Tobin. The 1962 *Economic Report* was a very important economic document. It had clearly signaled the views of major, mainstream economists' that economists had learned a lot on how to correct the errors that a free market might make and that governments no longer had excuses to not use that new knowledge, to bring the corrections, when these were needed and were demanded by the electorate. That trust in the available policy instruments was very different from the uncertainty that faces today's policymakers. By the way, the Council of Economic Advisers in those years reached a level of influence and prestige that is not imaginable today. During those years it was normal for its chairman to play tennis with the US President.

In the decades between the 1930s and the 1970s, the levels of taxes and of public spending grew significantly in all advanced countries, in some much more than in others. The share of taxes into GDP rose from an average of around 13 percent, at the beginning of the century, and a little higher before the First World War, to reach 30 or, in several countries, to exceed 40 percent of GDP in the early 1980s (see Tanzi and Schuknecht, 2000).

The use of regulations – not just to control the profits of monopolies, as at the beginning of the century, or to discourage alcohol consumption, as in the 1920s, but to reduce various new forms of negative externalities and potential abuses by individuals and enterprises – increased correspondingly, and so did the power and the role of labor unions. Labor unions had, first, become a powerful "counter-vailing power" (using an expression first used by J. K. Galbraith), to the economic power that the enterprises had had, and then had started to exercise an almost monopolistic power on their own.

The new urbanized setting in which many people now lived, and the growth of large cities in countries with deepening industrial activities, had made it more evident than in the past rural settings that some negative externalities (various forms of pollution, traffic congestion, non-hygienic behavior, excessive noises, some criminal activities, and others) needed to be controlled and that only governments could have the power to impose those controls. Environmental problems especially started to attract growing attention, and a book, *Silent Spring*, by sea biologist Rachel Carson (1962), that called attention to the contamination of rivers and springs, became a huge world bestseller.

The new regulations, the new spending programs, and the higher taxes continued to be criticized and opposed by libertarian or conservative economists, conservative politicians, and private enterprises. They would continue to advocate the virtues of small governments that, presumably, would leave individuals free in their actions and make economies more efficient.

The loss of "economic freedom," was rarely clearly defined, while the cost to enterprises of complying with the new regulations (that were often mentioned in the criticisms, and whose costs were estimated and often exaggerated by some conservative Think Tanks), were often mentioned and reported. The economic and social values of the regulations, on the other hand, were rarely estimated and were often challenged or minimized. The myth that the small government role would increase wellbeing continued to be popular in some groups.

The intervention by the government in those years became a big issue in attempts to regulate the use of tobacco, eliminate lead gasoline in cars, and to make cars more efficient in their fuel consumption. This was also the case when the government tried to protect springs and rivers from the effects of industrial pollution that was often killing all life in them. It has now become an issue in the use of dirty fuels that have been contributing to climate change.

The Great Depression had left deep scars in several countries, scars caused by the loss of incomes experienced by the unemployed workers and their families, at a time when there had been no formal safety nets and when the extended families (that had existed in the past and that had provided at least some primitive safety net for family members who were not capable of taking care of themselves) no longer existed. The large rural families had dispersed, due to the impact of the Industrial Revolution on the location of individuals of working age, and family links had weakened.

The Great Depression had created, or had increased, popular support for social programs and, also, for taxes based on the ability to pay, to finance those programs, especially the progressive personal income tax. In the United States and in the United Kingdom the marginal rates on the personal income taxes had been significantly increased, first in the 1930s, and then further, during the Second World War, when in the United States it reached 94 percent in 1944. With its progressive features, "personal income tax" had become an important source of revenue for the governments of many countries. In the United States, it had come to be considered an "ideal tax" in some surveys taken in the years after the war. It was "ideal" because it could provide revenue equitably and make the income distribution more equal, as many thought that it ought to do.

In the years between the war and the late 1960s, there had hardly been major concerns expressed by economists about the presumed negative effect that high marginal tax rates might have on personal incentives and on economic efficiency. The labor force participation had remained high in those years. These concerns would start being expressed in the second half of the 1970s and they would acquire popularity, mainly with the support of a curve – the *Laffer Curve* – a new concept that became both popular and a highly efficient propaganda tool used by conservative forces against almost any tax increase and against high tax rates and social programs. The Laffer Curve would acquire an important presence in any tax reform in the 1980s and in later years (see Tanzi, 2014a).

In the 1950s, a new tax that had been "discovered" and first introduced in France, the value added tax or VAT joined the arsenal of the tax tools available to governments. Over future years its use would spread rapidly among countries and it would join income tax as the major revenue source for most governments to raise revenue. This tax had come at the right time, because it could help finance the growing costs of the welfare programs that European countries and some other countries were introducing in those years.

The United States would not be among the countries that introduced VAT. Today, the United States is in an almost "splendid isolation" in *not* having a value added tax. In the United States, VAT had been opposed by both labor unions, as being particularly heavy on workers and poor families, and by local governments, because they were already taxing retain sales. Of course, it had been also opposed by libertarian economists, who have continued to oppose any new tax or any tax increase.

By not introducing a VAT, the US Federal Government would be forced to continue to rely on income taxes to finance public spending. Increasingly it would make use of "tax expenditures" to, presumably, promote social objectives, while keeping taxes and social spending lower than in other countries. Personal income tax has continued to provide about half of all US Federal revenue, while revenues from corporate income taxes have significantly fallen.

By not having a value added tax, and by using tax expenditures, the United States has kept its tax level significantly below that of other advanced countries, even though it spends far more than other countries for defense and a lot for Medicare and Medicaid. Today the United States has the lowest tax burden among advanced countries.

This has forced the United States to increasingly rely on public debt to finance its spending. This trend has been raising questions about the future sustainability of that debt, if interest rates should increase significantly and remain high in the coming years. The increase in 2022 forced the fast-rising inflation rate. Under current projections by the Congressional Budget Office, the share of the US public debt into GDP is expected to reach very high levels in future years.

10

The Conservative Counterrevolution

Until the early 1970s, the new social programs that had been introduced in the decades after the Second World War, financed by highly progressive taxes, combined with the power that the labor unions had acquired in earlier years, had led to significantly lower income inequalities as measured by Gini coefficients in the United States. They had also started to have negative effects on economic efficiency and on growth.

In the three decades after the end of the Second World War, the incomes of the citizens in the lower percentiles of the income distributions had increased significantly more than the incomes of individuals in the high percentiles. The goal of equity was being achieved. Around 1970 the share of labor income in total income had reached its highest level since the Second World War, about 63 percent. That share would fall to 59 percent by the mid-1980s and to 57 percent by 2011, due to the Great Recession of 2008–2010, that left many unemployed, and to the policy changes in the previous years. In the past, the share of labor income into national income had been considered (by major economists, such as Keynes, Kaldor, and Kuznets) to be broadly constant, fluctuating around a long-term trend. This was no longer the case in the recent decades, and labor had been the loser.

In the 1970s, in several countries, economic growth slowed down, or turned negative. In the late 1980s the incomes of individuals in the high percentiles started to grow at faster rates than the incomes of those in the lower percentiles. The Gini coefficients, that had been significantly reduced in the previous decades, until the mid-1980s, started rising. In the following two decades they would reach the high levels of a century earlier.

In the 1950s and early 1960s various policies had been introduced, aimed at assisting lower income groups, at protecting employment, at assisting larger families, and at providing some rights for dependent workers. In those years labor unions had acquired much more economic and political power. When combined with (a) the very high marginal tax rates on high personal incomes that prevailed at that time, (b) the high rates on corporate profits, and (c) the power of unions to push up real wages and other real workers' benefits, the policies had created reactions that reduced productivity. These effects would be especially pronounced in the United States, the United Kingdom, and other Anglo-Saxon countries.

In the late 1970s, those reactions would lead to changes in governments and policies. New conservative governments, especially in the United Kingdom and the United States, would try to reverse some of the policies of the previous decades. The changes would influence many countries, but, again, more the Anglo-Saxon countries.

The high *marginal* tax rates and the power that the labor unions had acquired in past years had probably gone too far, in what was still a capitalist world in which incentives mattered. In the 1960–1968 period, the lowest fifth of the real pre-tax, pre-transfer incomes of American families had seen real income growth at an annualized rate that was about double (6 percent) that for the other quintiles (about 3 percent). This result was extraordinary and not sustainable.

These factors would have negative impacts on economic performances and lead to reactions. In the United States and the United Kingdom, the policy reactions started coming in the late 1970s. They would intensify in the 1980s and expand to other countries. This would be important in a social environment that was rapidly becoming less pro-government and more pro-market.

The negative impacts of high tax rates and excessive union power had been attracting increasingly negative comments, first from conservative economists and politicians, then from an increasing number of mainstream economists and plain citizens, and especially from those who were paying the high tax rates and the media.

By the second half of the 1970s the negative impact on the economy of the past policies had become visible to many and, increasingly, it was being publicized by conservatives and started to lead to political reactions and the beginning of policy changes. This was happening at a time when countries had started to open-up their economies to competition from the rest of the world, so that the efficiency of the domestic economy had become more important.

Some abuses by overprotected union workers, especially but not only by those in public enterprises and publicly financed activities, including public railroads, public enterprises, and public-school systems, and economic rigidities created by the difficulties that the enterprises were having in adjusting the size of their labor force (by firing unneeded workers when necessary and by reducing high real wages, which were often indexed for inflation), had created additional economic distortions and were leading to increasingly negative commentaries, including in the media and, even, in the entertainment industry.

For example, a then popular song by the Beatles, titled *The Taxman*, had included the following lyrics: "I will tell you how it will be, one for you and nineteen for me, 'cause I'm the taxman." At the time the lyrics were written, the marginal tax rate on high incomes exceeded 90 percent in the United Kingdom. A British movie, titled *I am all-right Jack*, dealt with members of a labor union who were employed by a large, unionized enterprise. Because of the overprotection that was provided to the workers by the labor union rules, the workers received full wages, but many of them did little or no work and could not be fired. Frequently, some of them did not even show up for work or they spent the working day playing cards on the enterprise's ground.

There behaviors attracted increasingly negative reactions by the financial press and by economists, especially by those who had never liked the larger roles that governments and unions had assumed in the economy in the previous decades. The status of workers had clearly changed in those decades, from what it had been at the time of the *Papal Encyclical* in 1891, or even since the 1920s. It had gone from that of oppressed to that of oppressors, at least in the view of an increasing number of observers.

The fact that in the 1970s many countries were experiencing both high inflation and low growth, or even recessions at the same time, a combination that came to be called "stagflation," and that had not been considered possible by Keynesian economists, gave weight to these preoccupations that became increasingly widespread and started to be shared by the general public.

These reactions would lead to major political and economic changes in the 1980s and later years. By that time, questions were also being raised about the quality or the productivity of some, or much, public spending. See, as an example, *Unproductive Public Expenditure*, a pamphlet issued by the Fiscal Affairs Department of the IMF in 1995. That publication called attention to the low productivity of some public spending (see also Tanzi and Schuknecht, 2000) that argued that public spending beyond some limits (30–35 percent of GDP?) would be likely to become less productive or unproductive.

By the 1970s the Chicago School of Economics and the recently created School of Public Choice in Virginia had become influential players in the market for ideas. These "schools" were attracting an increasing number of followers to their conservative views, both among economists and among the better-informed citizens. By that time, Milton Friedman had become an important economist and a charismatic media personality. His very conservative views, often presented in a non-technical and colorful language that all could understand, were much listened to, especially his popular articles published regularly in *Newsweek*. They presented a new and presumably different world.

James Buchanan, the creator of the new School of Public Choice, had also become better known among a more academic group of economists, and not only in the United States. A new journal had been created to spread the *Public Choice* ideas. Both Friedman and Buchanan, and their followers, from different perspectives, believed in and promoted a limited economic role for the government and gave great importance to individual liberty, over behaviors constrained by community rules and goals or by altruism. Friedman's (1963) *Capitalism and Freedom* and Buchanan's (1975) *The Limits of Anarchy*, attracted many readers to their ideas. These books helped to spread the gospel of the merits of limited-government action.

11

Different Approaches to Social Protection

After the Second World War and, especially, in the 1960s, when the welfare states were being created in several countries, there was the beginning of a kind of bifurcation of the road toward their creation, with some governments of advanced countries taking alternative paths. Several of the continental European countries chose to raise their average tax levels by enough to finance, especially, some *universal* social programs, such as public health, education, general pensions, and some limited protection for the unemployed. The size of families also played a role in determining family allowances. These programs were made accessible and free, or accessible at highly subsidized rates, to all or to most citizens, regardless of the income levels of the beneficiaries.

The Scandinavian and some other European countries, such as France, Belgium, Austria, and others, chose this more "universal" route. Expenditure for social protection generally went up a lot in these countries to finance these programs (see Tanzi, 2011, table 12,1, p. 255). Public expenditure generally increased by around 20 percent of GDP. The "discovery" of value added tax in France in those years had provided a new and highly efficient source of tax revenue that these countries exploited.

Other countries, mostly the United States and, to a varying extent, other Anglo-Saxon countries, chose a more *"means-tested"* route, a route that allowed access to government programs only for citizens who met certain, well-specified, income levels or other eligibility criteria. These latter countries expected their citizens to rely more on their initiative and private insurances and less on government policies to help get some protection against several risks. These countries also made less or no use of the revenue generating possibility of value added tax.

The private insurance industry became a powerful lobby against the expansion of government programs in some countries and in some social areas, such as the provision of health. In the United States, today, one can buy private insurance even for one's funeral expenses. This private approach became especially important in the health sector and to a lesser extent in the educational and pension sector. It also became increasingly complex. In the Anglo-Saxon countries, the increase in social expenditure remained more contained than in some other countries. It was generally about 10 percent of GDP lower.

Universal programs tended to be more expensive but they were administratively and politically simpler because they required fewer decisions on admissibility and less administrative controls. They naturally required higher tax levels to finance them.

The means-tested programs were less expensive but required difficult political decisions on who could access them and were more complex to administer. Specific decisions on eligibility were needed and more administrative resources were required to determine who could benefit from them, to control the actual accessibility to the programs by the citizens, to prevent unauthorized use, and to reduce abuse. There is some evidence from a few countries, including the United States, that users that complained the most (the "squeaky wheels") would end up having more access to the public services. For example, it was recently reported that there are millions of Americans enrolled in Medicaid that should not be enrolled. The same is likely to have occurred for other programs.

The countries that relied on universal programs, generally, kept their tax systems less complex and more broad-based, to be able to more easily raise the higher revenue needed to finance the programs. For them the main objective of taxation remained that of generating the needed high revenue, while respecting some broad criteria of equity, neutrality, and simplicity in tax collection. The countries that relied on the means-tested programs generally chose, or ended up with, more complex and less neutral tax systems, in order to achieve, through the tax structures, rather than through public spending, the desired social objectives.

The countries that used universal programs made great use of the value added tax applied on as a wide base as possible, and of broader-based income taxes including, in the Scandinavian countries, "dual income taxes," a version of income tax that greatly simplified tax administration and tax filing on the part of taxpayers. The countries that chose means-tested programs relied more on income tax, using features such as "tax expenditures," "tax incentives," "special deductions," and other "tax breaks" in their tax systems that, with the passing of time, became increasingly more complex for taxpayers to navigate. Those that also used a value added tax used a much less broad-based version, using multiple rates and even a zero rate on some "necessary" items of consumption.

The "tax expenditures," or the "tax breaks," and the multiple rates for value added tax were designed to achieve some desired social objectives directly through the tax system, rather than to do it through the more resource expensive public spending programs.

For the United States, a country where citizens have always intensely disliked paying taxes, the choice of higher taxes was not welcome. As Eugene Steuerle, an economist at the Urban Institute in Washington, put it in his book (Steuerle, 1992), this is how "taxes came to dominate" the public agenda in the United States. They did it in a way that they had not in many other countries.

The use of "tax expenditure" had been suggested in the middle 1960s, in the US Treasury, by a tax lawyer from Harvard, Stanley Surrey, when he was Under-secretary in the US Treasury (see Surrey, 1973). Such specific use of tax expenditures had not been recognized before, although some tax breaks had always existed in the income taxes of various countries in past years, such as the personal exemption and deductions for dependent children, to reduce the tax burden in large families.

Tax expenditures were controversial from the beginning and they have remained controversial (see Weisbach and Nussim, 2004). They continued to be opposed by those who saw direct expenditures as being more effective in assisting those in need, and by those who pointed to the complications that tax expenditures created in the tax system (see Pechman, 1987, p. 357).

Tax expenditures would create an important "tax illusion" for citizens, an "illusion" of the type that the Italian economist Amilcare Puviani had written about, in an interesting book, first published in 1903. Tax expenditure could lower the need for higher public spending and for collecting higher tax revenue, policies that had continued to be strongly opposed and had been sharply criticized in the United States, and not only by conservative forces.

The introduction of income tax in the United States in 1913 had been strongly opposed and had required an amendment to the US Constitution before being introduced, even though only a few would pay it at the beginning because of the very high personal exemption. The year

1913 has been considered the beginning of the welfare state in the United States by some conservative economists. Some considered taxes as theft by governments, regardless of the use to which they were put. It was normal to want and to ask for more or better public services as long as they did not require higher taxes.

That need for the "fiscal illusion" created by the use of tax expenditures became particularly felt after 1965, because of the social legislation introduced in that year by President Johnson, "The War on Poverty," that would increase public spending and would require higher taxes to finance it, at a time when strong opposition to taxes, that in later years would become almost a "tax revolt," had started to materialize in California and other places. That opposition had already led President Kennedy to reduce the highest tax rate on income tax from 94 to 70 percent. The Vietnam War would soon create additional spending needs and create fiscal deficits that would lead to inflation.

The attraction of tax expenditures was that they made it possible to promote social objectives, in terms of income redistribution and social assistance, with less direct public spending and, thus, with a lower tax burden and tax rates. From a political point of view this seemed a clear win–win alternative for a country that seemed to be allergic to taxes, such as the United States. Tax expenditures would make an ideal use of Puviani's concept of "fiscal illusion." Like pizza, tax expenditures would be another Italian import that would prove highly popular in the United States; and, like pizza, they could come in many flavors. And more flavors could be added, as needed, over future years.

Tax expenditures could be provided as needed to both individuals and corporations, thus lowering the effective tax burdens on both. In future years corporations would benefit significantly from them. The contribution of corporate income taxes in GDP would become continually lower with the passing of the years.

Over the years, the demand for tax expenditures and the pressures to provide more of them would naturally increase, especially from those who had more resources to politically push for tax expenditures that would benefit them, mainly corporations, high net worth individuals, corporate managers, and well-funded vested interest, in particular areas and industries, such as petroleum and coal generation. For corporations, tax expenditures would create a real "corporate welfare system," one that, over the years, would significantly reduce the tax burden on corporations. Even the purchase of private planes by rich individuals or that of expensive electric cars by some rich individuals would in time benefit from tax breaks.

Just how popular tax expenditures, often called "tax breaks," would become can be assessed by using some recent information, provided by the Peterson G. Foundation, on August 19, 2020, and on March 29, 2022. According to that information, by 2019, the latest year for which data were available, there were more than 200 tax expenditures or tax breaks in the US tax system. They had reduced tax revenue by $1.6 trillion, or more than the United States spent on Social Security, on Defense, or on Medicare. Therefore, not only had the United States not introduced VAT to increase its tax burden to finance welfare spending it had also reduced the income taxes it collected to presumably deal with its welfare needs.

These tax expenditures, naturally, (a) violated the objective of tax neutrality, an objective that is so dear to economists, and created major distortions in the economy; (b) because of the complexity that they created, they increased the cost to taxpayers complying with their tax obligations; (c) the increase in the complexity of the tax system made it easier, especially for high income taxpayers, to evade or avoid the taxes that they should pay, and made the tax system less equitable (see Reid, 2017); and (d) they encouraged many able individuals to choose careers as tax consultants or lobbyists, rather than careers that would have been more beneficial to the welfare of the country's citizens.

According to the Peterson Foundation, in 2019, the eight most expensive tax expenditures were:

1. Exclusion from taxation (as incomes) of pension contribution and earnings – in 401(K)s and IRA programs – when these contributions are received. This exclusion that started as a small IRA account, in 1974, was increased by the employer-bases 401(K) in 1978 and grew over the years. Some have called it "the great American retirement fraud." By now, it has been estimated to be worth $250 billion. By 2019, 29 thousand taxpayers had accumulated IRA accounts that were each worth more than $5 million. Adding insult to injury, there have been continuous pressures to make it even more generous.

In 2022 a new bill called the "Securing Strong Retirement Act of 2022" received overwhelming approval by both political parties in Congress and, on October 23, 2022, the IRS raised the individual contribution from $20,500 to $22,500 as a compensation for inflation. That bill will make the exclusion more generous, starting in 2023, and, of course, the revenue loss to the Treasury even larger.

By the end of 2021 the assets in IRAs and 401(k)s combined had reached $21.6 trillion, providing handsome returns to those who manage them (see Hemel, 2022). As of 2018, 58 percent of wage earners made no contribution to these accounts, so the beneficiaries were largely those with higher incomes.

2. Reduced tax rates on dividends and on realized long-term capital gains. This tax break mainly helps wealthier individuals who receive dividends and have capital gains. It is estimated to cost the Treasury about $177 billion a year.

3. Exclusion from taxes of employees' contribution (what employers contribute) for medical insurance and care. This exclusion costs about $153 billion a year. It reduces the after costs of health insurance, but more for taxpayers in higher tax brackets. It clearly benefits insurance companies and higher income individuals.

4. Credit for raising children (child-care credit) that reduces the cost for families of raising children. It costs $118 billion a year. This tax expenditure is more helpful to low-income families.

5. Reduction in the tax rate on income received from controlled foreign corporations, which costs about $72 billion a year.

6. Tax subsidy for investment in equipment. This costs an estimated $72 billion a year.

7. Earned Income Tax Credit, available mainly to low-income parents. This is worth about $70 billion a year and is more favorable to lower income individuals.

8. Tax credits for health insurance bought through the marketplace. These cost about $53 billion a year.

The 200 or more "tax expenditures" or "tax breaks" that benefit mostly higher-income individuals and reduce tax revenue did not appear all at once. They were introduced gradually over the years. When they were introduced, many of them did not receive a full scrutiny of their costs and their incidence. Many had been strongly but discretely pushed by their sponsors and by the vested interests behind them and had not been strongly opposed by those who, in the long-term, would be the losers, the general public, due to their quiet introductions. The reason for the lack of attention was consistent with M. Olson's (1969) theory in his book *The Logic of Collective Action* that had theorized that when the losers are far less concentrated than the winners, and the issues are complex, the greater the concentration (i.e., the smaller is the number of beneficiaries), the greater will be the effort and the chance of winning, in a democratic setting.

Many tax breaks were introduced quietly and in the dark, and they received no or very little scrutiny when introduced. But they were strongly pushed, quietly and discretely, by those who would benefit the most from them or by their lobbies. The promoters of tax expenditures would exaggerate their social or economic merits, while they would minimize their costs, in both revenue and distortions. In many cases the general interest would pay little attention to these changes and it would end up being the affected and damaged loser who would pay the price in the long-term.

The direct beneficiaries of the tax expenditures were both low income and, especially, higher-income individuals and families. The tax expenditures included: *exclusions* of some sources of incomes from the taxable income; *deductions* of some expenses from the taxable income; dollar per dollar *credits* for some amounts spent; and *preferential tax rates* for some income sources, including unrealized capital gains. Some tax expenditures were against taxes on income, both personal and enterprise income, while others were against the payroll taxes (such as exclusion for health insurance and for pension and retirement accounts).

As to the beneficiaries from the tax expenditures, higher income taxpayers have tended to benefit far more in total amounts. They have received, in dollar terms, a larger absolute amount of the tax expenditures. Lower income taxpayers have received a far smaller absolute share of the benefits, but larger proportional shares, in relation to their lower, total incomes.

This tax expenditure route inevitably leads to many distortions, and to greater tax complexity that, over the years, significantly increases the economic costs to the economy and the tax compliance costs for most taxpayers, except for those who do not pay any income taxes. They must also reduce the growth of the economy, because of the distortions that they create.

These problems have become progressively more serious and more felt over the years and have elicited increasingly negative reactions from taxpayers, but at the same time they have led to additional requests for even more tax expenditures. Unfortunately, there are no countervailing forces that automatically fight the growth of the tax expenditures and of the tax complexity, as there are for direct public spending, and the prevailing anti-tax culture in the United States has continued to favor their use. The need to maintain equilibrium in the fiscal accounts has been a weak constraint in a period when real interest rates were low.

Commerce Clearing House, an institution that tracks tax developments every year "has estimated that there are about 420 significant changes in the tax code every year, [and] many ... require new forms, new rules and whole books of instructions for taxpayers to follow" (Reid, 2017, p. 215). The number of tax forms has increased enormously over the years, to accommodate the changes that are often well beyond the capacity of most normal citizens to understand and deal with. This trend has increasingly left the field open for specialists and for well-informed lobbyists to exploit. Increasingly they have led more and more taxpayers to rely on consultants, to prepare the tax declarations for them, leading to less and less knowledge of the tax systems by the citizens themselves. This is not a good development for a democracy that assumes that laws that are approved reflect the views of *knowledgeable* citizens.

The US tax code and the related regulations now require many tens of thousands of pages to describe the tax laws and the regulations, compared with a total of less than 500 pages that were required until the Second World War. The IRS now shifts most of the "compliance costs" on the taxpayers, while in some countries with higher tax levels, such as Sweden, Finland, and some others, taxpayers can prepare their tax declarations in a few minutes, using very simple forms. In some countries, the tax declarations of the taxpayers are even prepared by the tax administrations, which just sends them to the taxpayers for signing.

Some other countries, such as Italy, have learned the bad habit of using tax expenditures. For Italy, there are some estimates that report that the tax expenditures are about 600 and some economists have the dream of introducing flat taxes in this context. Would flat taxes eliminate the 600 existing tax expenditures before they are levied? Given that reality, the political talk of introducing flat taxes to make the system simple and the taxes efficient may make little sense.

As mentioned, the complexity of the tax system in the United States has forced many taxpayers, even low-income ones, to require the assistance of expensive tax consultants, thus creating another economic distortion and another potential lobby, the tax consulting industry. That industry must have acquired an interest in promoting the creation of additional complexity in order to increase its activity.

The tax consulting industry has been a major and growing one in the United States, and now hires many thousands of individuals to it. The cost of tax compliance has increased significantly as a share of GDP, but that cost is not shown in the countries' comparative statistics on tax burdens.

For all the above reasons, US taxpayers (and to some extent those in other Anglo-Saxon countries with broadly similar experiences, such as Australia) have felt over-taxed, even though their tax levels have not changed as much over the past half century and have remained significantly lower than those of several other advanced European countries.

In the United Kingdom in September 2022, the British Government proposed a significant tax cut in the middle of a major fiscal imbalance. This led to what should have been expected strong market reactions and political changes. The recently appointed Prime Minister would be forced to resign. For US high-income taxpayers, the tax burden has fallen since the mid-1980s and is now some 20 percent of GDP lower than that of several European countries. But complaints about high taxes and low public services continue. In the Anglo-Saxon countries, and especially in the United States, while the tax levels increased less than in most European countries over the past half century, the complaints about high taxes intensified, because of the increased complexity of the tax system, because of the high compliance costs that taxpayers have had to deal with and, possibly, because of cultural attitudes and some misreporting by the media.

Requests for the *earmarking* of public expenditures have also been a problem. About ten years ago, there had been an attempt to stop these requests, but recently they were again allowed, making the expenditure side of the budget much more complicated and inefficient than it should be.

Access by citizens to the benefits of means-tested programs tends to grow with time, because of political pressures by those who are excluded, bureaucratic maneuvers to make the programs more accessible, increasing abuses by citizens, and corrupt practices by some public employees. This has happened while Americans have continued to hate high taxes and explicit welfare payments, especially when they believe that the beneficiaries of the spending are mostly the lazy, while the taxes are paid by industrious and hard-working citizens. They do not see tax expenditures in the same way as direct welfare spending. Some tax experts have preferred to call them "tax aids" to stress the similarity. But many have continued to believe that "tax expenditures" are good and direct spending is bad, even when the budgetary impact is the same.

Racial prejudices and other biases have played some roles in these attitudes (see Gilens, 2014), as some surveys have indicated. These attitudes are limited to the spending side of the budget and not to the beneficiaries of the tax expenditures that are more difficult to identify and to connect with ethnic groups. Puviani's tax illusion has been at work and has been delivering the expected results.

Of course, means-tested programs may and occasionally do create some "poverty traps," because individuals on welfare who become employed lose access to the public subsidies, thus discouraging at least some of them from getting regular, but often, low paying jobs. These "poverty traps," which are often identified with poorer and often ethnically different groups, have attracted a lot of attention on the part of economists, especially by libertarian economists. They have contributed to the impressions that many Americans continue to have that those who get these targeted welfare benefits want to live at government's expenses. Wrong perceptions can easily lead to wrong policies

Some of these programs, of course, may create long-term dependency on them, may increase public spending, and may reduce economic efficiency and labor force participation. It is thus not surprising that poverty traps have attracted negative reactions by economists, perhaps more than they deserve, given their magnitude, and surely more than tax expenditures, some of which create comparable distortions. The poverty traps may be less important than people have been led to believe and their effects may be less damaging than those generated by some tax expenditures.

In the 1970s, taxes were still generally heavy, more progressive, and more complex than they had been before the Second World War in many countries – in some more than in others. They were creating possible disincentive effects for working taxpayers and some market inefficiencies. At the same time, the labor market had become overregulated and overprotected, due in part to the increased power of the labor unions and the number of workers who had joined them. Between 1964 and 1970, the output gap measured as a share of potential GDP had become negative. This would lead to the high inflation in the 1970s. It was also a time when the Vietnam war and the oil crisis were going on and were creating some deep divisions, and various countries were experiencing high inflation, high unemployment, and low or negative growth, a new, strange phenomenon called *stagflation* which conflicted with the so-called Philip Curve that had a large following among economists until that time.

These experiences led to growing concerns by many economists about some of the policies that were being followed, and growing opposition, to the high, progressive tax rates, to some of the social programs that had required the high tax rates and to the current role of the labor unions.

These reactions became especially strong in the Anglo-Saxon countries, the countries that had made more use of the means-tested programs, but they also affected other countries. The Scandinavian countries would react by introducing dual income taxes that reduced high marginal tax rates on incomes from capital sources, and by sharply reducing tax complexity. They also simplified their pension policies and reduced some public spending (see Tanzi, 2011).

The reactions to the welfare programs and to the work disincentive of taxes and welfare programs in Anglo-Saxon countries have been significantly different from those in the Scandinavian countries, perhaps, in part due to cultural factors and in part due to the choice of the instruments used to promote the social goals (see Atkinson and Mogensen, 1993). The disincentive effects seem to have been less important and to have attracted less reactions in the Scandinavian and in some other European countries, that had made more use of *universal* welfare programs, using more *broad-based* taxes.

By the second half of the 1970s, the potential disincentive effects of high marginal tax rates and of generous welfare programs, together with growing concerns about some inefficient use of resources, which had started to be widely reported by the media, some abuses of means-tested programs, and concerns about the role that labor unions had been playing, especially in some areas (public schools, public enterprises and in large, unionized private enterprises), were being publicized by conservative groups and were influencing public opinion, especially in the United States and the United Kingdom. This change in opinions would lead to the election of very conservative and articulate leaders, including, in the United Kingdom, Margaret Thatcher, and, in the United States, Ronald Reagan.

Clearly the equilibrium, or the harmony between the desired role of the market and that of the government, that had seemed to have been achieved in the mid-1960s, had been broken. This new situation would require major adjustments in policies, aimed at reducing the government role and at increasing that of the market, in order to bring, again, more harmony between the two. In the early 1980s an output gap as large as 6 percent of GDP would be necessary to kill the inflationary pressures.

The decades that followed would be characterized by what came to be called "market fundamentalism" or "supply side economics" or even "Washington Consensus." It was a "fundamentalism" that would change both policies and, perhaps even more importantly, attitudes, about the role of the government and that of the market and about the expected results that a free market could generate. It would also challenge the legitimacy and the popularity that the "Keynesian Revolution" had acquired in the earlier decades, shifting attention, for the stabilization of the economy, from fiscal to monetary policy.

Monetary policy would play the leading role in the years that followed, while the use of fiscal policy for stabilization would be downplayed. That change would bring different kinds of potential instability, which would be discovered during the Great Recession of 2009 and again during the inflation of 2022.

12

The Economy in the 1970s

Before we focus on the world that the new century would bring, it may be useful to review briefly the economic situation that had developed in the decade of the 1970s, after the large expansion of the government role in past decades and after other developments that had preceded it. By the beginning of the 1970s, there were clear signs that some of the changes that the policies of recent decades had generated had changed the existing economies in some fundamental and not always desirable ways, because some of the policies that had been introduced had clearly gone too far in a market economy.

The negative signs were not necessarily related to those that had come from the pressures directed at changing the role of the state to promote a more equal distribution of income, as reported in earlier chapters. The problem was in part in the way that role had been promoted and in how some policies had influenced the private economy. Although it is difficult to identify with precision the main changes that may have had the most potentially negative impact on future developments, some follow here.

First, there were the beginning signs of the opening of global markets, especially the markets for many of the goods that people needed and bought. Various countries had started to open their frontiers to foreign trade, by lowering import duties, removing some import restrictions, and by making it easier to import cheaper products that had previously been domestically produced. The opening of trade relations among countries accelerated during the 1970s and 1980s, and it led to large increases in the share of imports in the countries GDPs and other changes.

While in principle the opening of domestic markets was a desirable development and was supported by most economists, because it lowered the prices of some products for the consumers of the importing countries and increased the efficiency in the use of the world productive resources, it also challenged the jobs of some industrial workers in the importing countries, thus negatively affecting the economic conditions of those workers who had been engaged in the production of some of the now imported goods. In other words, it created a *distributional* problem. This change was coming at a time when government programs to assist the damaged workers were being removed and the prevalent view was that the unemployed workers should not be assisted.

The prevailing thinking, strongly supported by the currently developing market fundamentalist philosophy, was that the natural mobility that exists within a freer market economy would allow the workers who lost their jobs to easily move to where better jobs were becoming available in the expanding export activities. Therefore, there was no need for the government to intervene. The market would take care of the problem.

The opening of foreign markets, that was expected by many economists to lead to a more efficient world economy and more growth, would create the phenomenon of deindustrialization in some prevalently industrial countries, including the United States and the United Kingdom. It would lead to the economic decline of previously affluent regions and cities, as, for example, would happen in Michigan and Detroit, and some other areas in the United States (see Bluestone and Harrison, 1982).

The fast growth of China, India, Vietnam, Bangladesh, South Korea, and other countries in those years would accelerate this process. These countries would become major exporters and producers of some of the goods that had been previously produced and even exported by the industrial countries. Some of the previously poor countries would become the major beneficiaries of the trade liberalization policies, because their growth rates would increase.

Second, and closely connected with the first development, there was the creation of new multinational corporations, enterprises that operated in several countries and that were not engaged mainly in the production of raw materials, such as oil, copper, iron, aluminum, etc., and mainly in colonial countries, as they had been in the past. The new, multinational corporations, which responded less to the policies of single countries, were often engaged in the production of the same consumer goods, such as automobiles, home appliances, clothes, shoes, and toys that previously had been produced in the advanced countries.

The new multinational enterprises could use the cheap capital and the advanced technologies available in their residence countries and combine them with the cheap labor of the developing countries to produce, more cheaply, many of the same goods that consumers wanted everywhere.

At some point, this process went so far as to give one the impression that everything that one bought in the United States and in other advanced countries came from China. China became the country where many goods were assembled and from where they were exported, even when they were not entirely produced there. China would soon become a major economic power, competing with the more traditional powers, first Japan and then, especially, the United States. In this period there would be "hearings" in the US Congress to determine how to deal with this form of "global reach." What should the US policy reaction be? In a world where market fundamentalism was becoming dominant, the answer was that no policy reaction was needed. The freer market would deal with the problem, as it was expected to deal with many other problems.

The workers who lost their jobs had the "freedom" to move to the places where better jobs were available, if their skills, finances, and family circumstances allowed them to. The government had no business to intervene and, in the United States and United Kingdom it generally did not intervene, either with job training or with financial assistance. Therefore, the process of deindustrialization started, intensified over the years, and continued to take place, leading to future difficulties.

Third, while in the past trading had taken place mainly in tangible commodities, there were signs of growth in the international trading of some services, from tourist to educational services, and even to some health services. Hundreds of thousands of Chinese, Indians, Koreans, and other students went to study in foreign universities, absorbing technical knowledge and bringing it back to their countries, thus reducing the initial technological gap that had existed between developed and some previously developing countries.

Foreign tourism, and the industries associated with it, grew rapidly in those years and tourism became an important economic activity in many countries, creating many jobs and generating much income. It was also promoted by the rising incomes some countries, that had been damaged by the Second World War, had witnessed in the previous decades, which had been characterized by "economic miracles" and by the fast growth of some previously poor countries, such as China, that were creating a more affluent and educated middle class among their large populations. It was also promoted by falling transportation costs and by the desire on the part of better educated populations, increased by the afterwar "baby boom" and by rising incomes, to see more of the world in which they lived.

The faces of foreign tourists would no longer be mostly American, as they had been in earlier decades. They would increasingly become cosmopolitan faces. Even the production of new books would be affected. New books, published in the United States or the United Kingdom, would often be edited and printed in India, due to the lower costs in that country. These were aspects of a globalizing economy.

Fourth, there was the opening of the financial market, a market which had been close until the recent past. Until the 1970s, financial markets had been mainly national and, in the United States, even confined mainly to single states, because commercial banks had been allowed to operate only in the states where they were chartered. There had been a sharp separation between the activities of "commercial banks" and those of "investment banks" and, in the 1970s, there had not yet been many activities promoted by legitimate, as distinguished from illegal, "shadow banking" activities.

There had not been "hedge funds" in the past, institutions that dealt with "derivatives," and there had not been "credit swaps." Exchanges across countries had required difficult transactions and so had large financial operations, such as the buying of, or the investing in, foreign enterprises. Legal "shadow banking" activities would explode in later years, increasing the numbers of people who worked in those activities, and allowing credit to move around at increasing speed and amount, and with less and less resistance. Good information would acquire more value in this new world. Cross-countries payments would become much easier in the years that followed. Moves by individuals from financial activities to high government jobs and vice versa would also become a more common phenomenon.

In the 1970s, individuals had the choice between "checking accounts" and "saving accounts," both held in "commercial banks," until "certificate of deposits" of fixed maturity and interest rates became common for personal savings. In later years many other investment opportunities, such as indexed funds, would become available for individuals, beside the option of buying company shares directly from the stock market, an option that had always existed, but had become easier. Attempts to beat the market would proliferate at times with the use of inside information.

There were no credit cards yet, and people who had to travel to foreign countries had to procure the needed foreign exchange before leaving their countries; or to buy "travelers checks" from institutions such as Thomas Cook or American Express. Once one was in a foreign country, it was both expensive and time consuming to change dollar bills into the needed local currency for domestic transactions. In many countries one could be arrested for attempting to leave the country with dollar bills in one's pockets. And, in some countries, it was difficult to acquire foreign exchange. In some countries, black markets offered illegal and potentially dangerous options.

While the above liberalizing changes were going on, there were other developments that were creating some difficulties for the operations of the national economies of advanced countries. The decade of the 1970s experienced a long period of high inflation, combined with low productivity growth, high unemployment, and low or even negative economic growth in several countries. The unusual combination of inflation and recession, taking place at the same time, was one which had seemed to be highly unlikely to Keynesian economists. It came to be called "stagflation," a process that would last for a full decade, until 1982, when Paul Volker, the then Chair of the Federal Reserve, put a stop to it by sharply increasing the Federal funds effective interest rates to 19.25 percent and creating a recession for a few years.

The 1970s would also see the collapse of the Bretton Woods agreements on exchange rates and the end of the gold standard by the United States. The dollar would become the world currency and many central banks would now hold dollar balances rather than gold balances.

The great power that the labor unions had acquired in the previous years had led to abuses on the part of some of their members and to increasing economic inefficiencies for countries, due to those abuses. Labor unions would be partly blamed for the economic situation that prevailed in the 1970s, because they had promoted excessive growth in real wages and had allowed various abuses by workers that, through a cost-push dynamic, had led to low productivity growth and high inflation.

The power of the unions would start to decrease in the late 1970s, in part due to actions by the administrations of Margaret Thatcher in the United Kingdom and Ronald Reagan in the United States, and would continue to decrease until the 2000s. In the more recent years, it has started to increase again (see Yeh, Macaluso, and Hershbein, 2022). Today, the power of unions is in in ascendency in various areas (transportation, health, etc.) reflecting the dialectic behavior of capitalist economies, which periodically see these changes. Future years are likely to witness more strikes and more pushes for higher wages, promoted by labor unions.

It seemed that the goal of more equality in the income distribution, and the creation of safety nets for individuals and families, sought in the years after the Second World War, had been achieved, in part, at the cost of economic efficiency. The harmony that should have existed between the two objectives, and that many believed had been achieved, or at least approached, in the mid-1960s, was no longer there. Greater equality was being achieved but at the cost of too high inflation and low efficiency and growth.

The energy crisis in the 1970s had been caused mostly by political developments, in Iran and other places. It had sharply increased the price of petroleum and had been one of the contributors to the high inflation, which had further been promoted by the low real interest rates, until the rates were sharply raised by the action of the Federal Reserve in the United States, in 1982, before the US economy and those of other countries would start growing again, under different policies

The 1970s had also seen higher fiscal deficits, due to the Vietnam war, and increasing disagreements on policies to pursue, among other political problems (Watergate scandal, the fixing of some prices, etc.). The Keynesian orthodoxy would be subjected to heavy criticism.

All these factors had combined and contributed to create reactions, especially by libertarian economists who had continued to have high faith in the operations of the free market and low faith in those of the government. These economists had started to call for a return to pro-market and more laissez faire policies and their calls had started to attract more followers and to contribute to the creation of an intellectual atmosphere that would lead to the market fundamentalist policies of the 1980s and of later years. There were of course contrasting evaluations of the impact of the welfare programs in the United States and United Kingdom in the previous years. For the United States, some can be read in the exchange between Tobin and Wallis (1968).

The decades that followed the 1970s would not only reduce the role that the government (and the labor unions) had been playing in the economy in the previous decades but, for various reasons, they would also radically transform the structures of the economies. In that transformation, services and the exchange of information would grow in importance, compared to the production and the exchange of hard goods. The importance of "intellectual property" and of good information would grow, compared with that of real property.

The role played by the "publicness" of some goods and services would grow in importance, with significant distributional implications for the economy. That role will be discussed in Part III, with other developments that would characterize and dramatically change the world in the decades that followed. In those decades the policy changes would take place at broadly the same time as a major technological revolution. To a considerable extent it would be a revolution from the use of steel to that of silicon. The increasing use of *semiconductors* would come to define the new era.

PART III

THE PERIOD AFTER THE 1970S

13

A Return to Laissez Faire?

Chapter 12 covered the decade of the 1970s, a decade that experienced the Vietnam War, a sharp rise in oil prices, high inflation, low economic growth, and high unemployment. It had not been a good period for many countries' economies, including the United States and United Kingdom, or for many citizens. In that decade, the United Kingdom had experienced the highest inflation in its whole history, and it had been forced to go to the International Monetary Fund (IMF) for a large stabilization loan.

For various reasons, 1968 had been a particularly turbulent year for several countries but it had followed several, relatively good years. The 1970s also signaled the end of some "economic miracles," periods of fast economic growth, in several countries, that had characterized the two decades after the Second World War and had much increased the GDPs and the per capita incomes of several important countries, including Japan, Germany, Italy, and others, countries that had been much damaged by the Second World War.

In the 1970s, several prominent, conservative, or libertarian economists (Hayek, Friedman, Buchanan, Lucas, Stigler, Becker, and some others) had become better known in the economic profession and some even to the wider public, thus becoming more influential than previously. The writings or the public declarations of these economists started to attract more attention and larger followings to their pro-market and anti-government views, even among less conservative or less libertarian economists.

Many economists had not been happy with some of the ongoing economic developments, including the high political power that labor unions had acquired and the use they were making of that power. They were also not happy with the very high marginal tax rates that, when combined with the high inflation in those years, were pushing many individuals into high tax burdens, in a process that was called "fiscal drag" (see Tanzi, 1981).

The *Chicago School of Economics*, the *School of Public Choice*, and to a lesser extent *the Austrian School* became influential players in the market for ideas, far more than they had been in the previous decades, that had been largely monopolized by the Keynesian Revolution, pro-government views, and the creation of welfare states.

These conservative or libertarian "schools" created strong academic followings and formed growing opposition to the high taxes, the regulations, and the welfare programs introduced in the previous decades. Some defenders of the *status quo* would argue that these schools were creating the equivalent of economic religions. However those schools started to attract larger followings to their views, in some countries more than in others.

From different perspectives, in those years Buchanan and Stigler would argue that the demand for government intervention and regulations was largely determined by a "political market," a market in which, in a democracy, various political influences determined the votes of the citizens. In that political market, interest groups would push the governments to promote policies that would benefit the members of groups and not necessarily the general interest.

These economists stressed the importance of *individual* rights and the economic freedom of individuals, as compared with those of groups or communities. They claimed that the above rights had been ignored in the previous decades, when excessive importance had been given to presumed, community or social rights (see Buchanan, 1975; Stigler, 1975). The implication was that the restorations of *individual* rights could come only by reducing the role of the government in the economy.

Milton Friedman's (1963) book, *Capitalism and Freedom*, that had been published a decade earlier, and that stressed the link between capitalism and individual freedom, attracted continued attention. That book had made a strong defense of economic liberty and of how that liberty was an essential part of capitalism. It had argued that the pursuit of self-interest by free individuals and by enterprises, in a free market, would lead to the improvement in welfare *for everyone*, even when the individual agents ignored social considerations in their personal behavior, but respected some limited and widely agreed behavioral norms.

Hayek's works also attracted more attention and more readers in favor of free markets, although in his later works he had recognized the need for some minimum, essential government role in free markets, as for example in pollution control, and had stated that he was *not a conservative* and was ready to accept changes, when the changes were justified (Hayek, 1960; see also Miller, 2010; and Tanzi, 2015).

Hayek's qualifications would generally be ignored by his many conservative followers, and many continued to see his views through the narrow perspective of his 1944 book, that had warned about the "road to serfdom" represented by the Marxist, Russian style alternative, in which the role of the market had been largely abolished. That book had sold hundreds of thousands of copies, many in Special Abridged Editions, and had been very influential when first published.

In the 1970s, some of these conservative economists had promoted, or had given intellectual support, to a few real life experiments which reflected their economic, pro-market ideas. These experiments were then undergoing in Chile, under a military dictatorship, or in jurisdictions such as Hong Kong and Taiwan. Those experiments were presented as ideal economic models for the rest of the world to follow, models of how economies should be run. Those models would have some impact on policies in other countries, in part because some of the policies were endorsed by some international organizations, such as the World Bank.

The policies that the "Chicago Boys" were promoting in Chile in those years were highly advertised and much admired, such as the privatization of the public pension system, that would become a model for other countries, and be promoted by the World Bank: and the privatization of many previously public activities, including that of some major infrastructures which was followed by many countries. However, some well-informed Chilean, and more mainstream economists, would remain unimpressed by these policies that were promoted by an authoritarian government (see, e.g., Solimano, 2012).

The Chilean experiment would bring higher economic growth to that country for many years, but less equity. In later years, less conservative governments would be elected and would start to reverse some of the more conservative policies.

Public–Private Partnerships (PPPs) would become common experiences in those years, in the building of major infrastructures in many countries. In these, the financing of the infrastructures would come from private sources, thus reducing the need for governments to raise taxes, or to borrow, and fees would be charged for the use of the infrastructures. This would have clear, short run financial benefits for governments. In some countries these PPPs would put governments at fiscal risks of contingent liabilities, when unanticipated events, or at times nontransparent acts of corruption in the initial contracts, would create results which were different from the expected ones. In several countries governments would be forced to intervene, with taxpayers' money, to sustain the infrastructure (see Polackova-Brixi and Schick, 2002, for some evidence of this).

In the second half of the 1970s, due to the depressed state of many economies, the pursuit of economic efficiency moved up in importance, in the view of an increasing number of economists, while the pursuit of equity, which had required some significant redistribution of income and wealth in previous years, started receiving less support. The pursuit of equity and of income redistribution started to be considered, by some important economists, as a dangerous distraction from that of efficiency, as Lucas would forcefully state at that time. Margaret Thatcher and Ronald Reagan and some other political leaders would endorse these conservative views and play major roles in converting them into policies, after their elections.

In those years, some presumed government failures started to be widely reported and publicized, and, in some cases, exaggerated by the equivalent of what may at times have been *fake news*. There was, for example, the story, told by Ronald Reagan, of a beauty queen who was reported to go to collect her unemployment check in a Cadillac. True or false, that story attracted a lot of attention, as did the stories of individuals who received food stamps from the US government, because of their low income, but used the stamps to buy alcoholic beverages instead of food. Both these conservative, political leaders (Thatcher and Reagan) set out to reduce the role of the government in their respective countries in the years that followed.

In those years, welfare payments came to be seen by some as promoting laziness and damaging personal incentives, and they were sharply criticized. And so were high tax rates, that presumably made individuals choose leisure over work. Those receiving the welfare payments were increasingly seen as lazy individuals unwilling to work, who wanted to enjoy a life of leisure at government expense, that is at the expense of the hard-working and tax paying individuals. The welfare recipients were often individuals from minority groups, including immigrants.

On August 12, 1986, President Ronald Reagan would famously state that: "The nine most terrifying words in the English language are: *I am from the government, and I am here to help.*" This statement summarized the current view among conservatives about the role of the government, and indirectly about the positive view of the role that a free market could play in promoting general welfare. It also raised the more fundamental question about whether a government was at all needed, in a country with a free market economy, where the market was assumed to be able to do almost anything.

Over the years, some important philosophers and social scientists, such as Wilhelm Ropke (2006), Julian LeGrand (1991), Bertrand de Jouvenel (1952), Richard Pipes (1999), Robert Nozick (1974), Lacey (2001), and others, had contributed to this thinking, a thinking that had stressed individual freedom and responsibility over collective equity and assistance, and that reflected a deep distrust of collective action and of governments.

As de Jouvenel put it: "redistribution is in effect far less a redistribution of free income from the richer to the poorer … than a redistribution of power from the individual to the state." This had become a common view. Fear of an over powerful state was behind these views and worries, because, in the distant past, the state had, often, not been democratic but created a monopoly with the focus of power belonging to a few, limiting the power for the rest (see Gordon, 1999). This has also happened more recently, in socialist countries.

Historically, there had not been an equal fear about the overwhelming power that rich individuals, even when not directly representing the government through their birth rights or other government provided privileges, might assume in countries with democratic institutions and market economies, because of their great wealth and the use that they made of it.

This, however, has started to happen in some countries, where some individuals had acquired huge wealth and, because of that wealth, they had acquired much indirect power. In the past individuals had not had power that had been separate from the one obtained from the state. This had been the case with members of the nobility. Therefore, the view was that only the state could monopolize power.

The influence of libertarian views became particularly strong in the countries where the social programs, which had been introduced in the previous decades, had been "means-tested" and thus had focused on specific and easily identifying categories of citizens. That is, they had been, in intention at least, limited to individuals who officially could be identified as poor and in need of assistance, as had been the English Poor laws that had existed in England since Queen Elizabeth I.

Although over the years, and for a long time, many countries had used *some* means-tested programs to assist a few individuals in special cases, that is individuals who were clearly unable to earn an income, these means-tested programs had been especially used and welcomed in Anglo-Saxon countries, and particularly in the United States. These programs had put the individuals who received government assistance in special and easily identifiable categories.

Some or many of the beneficiaries of the welfare programs inevitably belonged to minorities, including racial minorities, widows or unmarried women with children, and immigrants, and, because of the low wages that they often received when they worked, they had less of an incentive to look for jobs that would make them lose their welfare benefits, as long as those benefits were available. Naturally, given the alternative, some of them preferred to remain on welfare, if they could. This helped create the bad reputation that the welfare programs acquired in these countries.

This bad reputation was not extended to the less visible and less identifiable recipients of the "tax expenditures" that especially helped tax paying individuals. The tax expenditures absorbed large parts of the potential budget, more than the welfare payments did, but they were less visible. The beneficiaries of the tax expenditures were generally seen as respectable, middle or higher-class individuals. They were for the most part not minorities.

In those earlier years, the income taxes used to pay for the welfare programs still had high marginal rates, so that the tax expenditures had high values for the taxpayers who benefitted from them. The higher was their income, the greater was the value of the tax expenditure.

The use of "tax expenditures" also started to create complexity in the tax system, thus increasing compliance costs for many taxpaying individuals, which made the taxes paid appear more burdensome to them. These individuals were likely to consider the tax expenditures which benefited them fair and justified. They did not see them as part of the welfare system, as they came to consider the direct benefit payments to the "lazy" welfare recipients. This problem would intensify with time. The Puviani "tax illusion" had worked as some had expected it would work. It had created an intended, or perhaps not fully intended for some, fiscal illusion,

Some important, strongly opinionated and articulate political figures, such as Margaret Thatcher, Ronald Reagan, and others, who had won, or would win, the elections in their countries in those years, did not see the government as a potentially useful and compassionate actor, one that could complement the work of the market, bringing to it some necessary corrections and equity, as it had been seen in the 1950s and the 1960s. Rather they saw it as an enemy of the market and of the capitalist system.

For these political figures, the government had become a break on, or even a killer of, the capitalist system. It had become a Leviathan monster, a monster that had to be controlled before it swallowed everyone, as Hobbes had feared that the government could do centuries earlier or as it had done in Russia and in Socialist countries.

At the same time, the market was being advertised as an efficient and almost miraculous instrument, one to be admired and used, and, especially, one that could efficiently solve many of the social and economic problems that afflicted many citizens. However, they argued that constraints on the market imposed by governments in previous decades, such as high taxes and regulations, had to be removed, or at least drastically reduced. Some formal economic theory developed around these beliefs, and policies followed them.

The economic difficulties that the "centrally-planned" countries, the countries that had been part of the Soviet Union, were encountering in those years, provided a convenient contrast to the proposed free markets, as were the favorable experiences of Hong Kong and the more recently introduced one of Chile. The problems that freer markets had faced in the years before the war had, by then, been largely forgotten, or had never been internalized. The present is often more influential than the past. A new and promising world had seemed possible – a world that could make everyone both more prosperous and, especially, freer.

An increasing number of economists and even of plain citizens came to see the choice as a simple one: between an efficient, capitalist system, with a free market, individual freedom, low taxes, and few regulations, that would create prosperity and increase the freedom and the wellbeing of most citizens, and one close to the planned and failing economies of Soviet Union countries, with controlled markets, low or no individual freedom, high implicit or explicit taxes, many regulations, scarcity of many products, and little economic progress.

Middle grounds alternatives were not contemplated or considered. No "third ways" were considered possible, only corner solutions. The choice was presented as that between the extreme alternatives of central planning, Soviet style, on one side, and libertarian, free economies, on the other. Given this choice, who would choose central planning?

In those years, some old and some new theoretical economic concepts, such as "The Ricardian Equivalence," "Rational Expectations," "Efficient Markets," "Excess Burden," "Optimal Market Allocation," "Laffer Curve," and others attracted increasing followings among academic economists, and even among some politicians who thought that they had a good understanding of how economies really worked. Some of these politicians became vocal in promoting the new gospel, and the listed theories were given more weight than they may have deserved.

Some influential newspapers and magazines, especially the *Wall Street Journal* and even *The Economist*, joined the debate, mainly on the side of the free market, as did some old or newly-created "Think Tanks." Some of the latter would become increasingly influential and would reflect the strong political biases of their staff and of those who financed them, in their research and publications activities. They would find little difficulty in financing their activities, in the new climate that was creating many new rich individuals, who naturally wanted to protect and increase their wealth.

Many of the leading conservative economists of those years – Friedman, Hayek, Buchanan, Stigler, Lucas, Becker, Mundell, etc. – would earn Nobel Prizes in Economics, indicating that even the members of the Nobel Prize Committee at the Swedish Central bank had been impressed by the new economic ideas, which were also having, or would have, some impact on the policies of European and other countries, including Canada, Australia, New Zealand, and even the Scandinavian countries (see Tanzi, 2011).

The Nobel Prizes in Economics would give additional visibility and prestige to these conservative or libertarian economists and would help them attract more public attention to their ideas. Surely, some must have thought, so many Nobel Prize Winners in Economics could not be wrong! By 2022, eighty-three individuals had won these prizes, and thirty-one of them went to individuals somewhat associated with the University of Chicago. The Nobel choices would become increasingly controversial over the years, and some of the winners would quickly disappear from visibility.

In some ways and to some extent, in those years, we all became, at least a little, followers of Milton Friedman and more libertarian than we had been. The current climate was pushing everyone in that direction.

Friedman's book, *Capitalism and Freedom*, that had been published in 1962, became one of the most read and cited books in economics, and Adam Smith's "invisible hand" became a very active and very "visible" hand in many discussions, even though Adam Smith himself had mentioned it only in passing, and without giving it much emphasis. Greed would become a virtue in those years, and poverty would become a moral defect that was assumed to say much on the character of the poor persons, regardless of the real causes of their poverty.

By the second half of the 1970s, the political winds had clearly changed direction, from those that had been blowing in favor of the larger government roles in the previous decades, to those that favored less government and more market. The new winds were creating increasingly skeptical attitudes toward the large economic role that the government had assumed in the past decades, and toward many of the social programs that had been introduced.

The new winds had created a much more favorable attitude toward a freer, unregulated economy, and the ground had become ready for the pro-market revolution that would come, fully, in the 1980s and the following decade, in several countries. It would be called "market fundamentalism" or "supply-side economics."

It was a return to the old view that, in a free economy, the supply creates its own demand. Therefore, there is no need for stabilization fiscal policies. In a flexible and free market, when there is a supply, there will always be a demand for it, and jobs would be created for those willing to work *at the offered wages*. Therefore, wages needed to be flexible. In ideological terms, it would be almost a return to the 1920s, or even to a century earlier when J. B. Say and his "Say's Law" had first been announced. This new government role would contrast sharply with the pro-government bias, the great emphasis on the demand side of the economy that had characterized the economic policies during the years of the Keynesian Revolution, and the welfare reforms that had been introduced in the years until the 1960s.

In the new environment, the supply-side, or the market fundamentalist revolution, played a role in the election of highly conservative and eloquent policymakers in several countries (United Kingdom, United States, Canada, Australia, New Zealand and others, even in Italy in 1994). "Market fundamentalism" became a popular ideology even among much of the general public, which was not likely to have understood its full implications.

In spirit, it could be seen as a return to the laissez faire ideology that had prevailed a century earlier. However, it had become more of a free choice for governments than it had been in the earlier period, when the likely alternative had been some forms of mercantilism and not the modern welfare state. That mercantilist alternative has continued to exist today, in some less developed and corrupt countries, including Russia.

In the 1980s and the 1990s many economists came to believe that the free market, unassisted by government action, and unimpeded by it, could solve many economic and social problems if it were allowed to operate freely. High marginal tax rates and many regulations came under strong attack, because they were assumed to restrict the market and to significantly reduce the incentives and the economic liberty of individuals. Support for low and even for "low and flat taxes" increased. Thatcher, who would liberalize and transform the British economy in those years, would even try to introduce a poll tax, one that was to be collected in equal amount from everyone, rich and poor, ignoring ability to pay. The view was that all citizens should pay for the financing of the essential state and not mainly the better to do. The push for this tax would be Thatcher's undoing. She had clearly tried to go too far to the right and many citizens had refused to follow her.

Some of the conservative ideas, in the 1990s, would be sold to countries that were coming out of central planning, the so-called transition economies (see Kornai, 1992; Tanzi, 2010). They would also be sold to some developing countries. It is an open question as to the effect that they have had on those countries.

14

The Policies of Market Fundamentalism

Tax Reforms, Globalization, and Deregulation

An early and important effect of the change in intellectual climate was on tax rates. In the United States, until 1978, the highest marginal tax rate on personal income had been 70 percent. That rate was reduced to 50 percent in 1982–1986 (see Pechman, 1987). The US "Fundamental Tax Reform" of 1986, introduced by the Reagan Administration, would dramatically reduce the US Federal, marginal tax rates on personal income for later years, and would also try to reduce the "tax breaks" that had been introduced in the two previous decades. It would be successful in the first objective but not in the second. The rates were reduced, the highest rate of personal income to only 28 percent. However, many of the tax breaks, or tax expenditures, remained, or quickly returned. New ones would soon be added. A few years later, some increase in the rates would become necessary, because of growing fiscal deficits. It should be recalled that the highest tax rate for personal income tax had exceeded 90 percent during the Second World War and for many years after the war, until the Kennedy years.

Remarkably, the 1986 reform was not strongly opposed by the liberal political forces that still existed at that time and became the law. President Reagan and the head of the Democratic Party in the House of Representatives still had a good enough personal relation at that time to play golf together. The personal relations between people had still not been much affected by the new climate, as they would be in later years. People could disagree on policies but still remain friends

Given the international importance of the United States, the US tax reform would have a strong demonstration effect on other countries, leading to domino rate reductions in many of them and, as a consequence, increasing tax competition among countries (see Wunder, 2001). Tax competition in a more globalized environment makes it easier for some taxpayers to escape high rates by changing location, without necessarily changing activity. This gives some empirical content to the Laffer Curve, a content that it would not have in the absence of tax competition.

Over the years after 1986, the US tax reform would lead to increasing tax competition among countries, and to attempts by multinational corporations and "high net-worth individuals" to reduce their tax payments by moving and thus changing residence. Early discussions of these effects can be seen in Gravelle (1986) and Tanzi (1987, 1995).

Tax competition and tax avoidance have remained significant problems without solution until now. They are still awaiting internationally agreed solutions, which are difficult because of the conflicting objectives and the different ideologies between countries. Tax competition exists also between US states which, to a large extent, makes it easier for some individuals or enterprises to escape higher tax rates, by moving to another state. High income individuals may move from, say, New Jersey to Florida, or from Norway to Switzerland, because of tax reasons, as some billionaires have done in recent years, In the United States, some athletes have been taking tax factors into considerations when choosing the team where they would play.

In the 1980s and the 1990s the economic role of governments was reduced in many countries. Some economies became less regulated and, increasingly, more globalized and more financially leveraged. The financial market became less regulated, credit became more easily available from global sources, and monetary policy, often promoted with low interest rates, became more important than it had been, replacing the role that fiscal policy had played.

After the early 1980s, US nominal interest rates fell on average by several percentage points, and the 1990s was generally a good decade in terms of economic performance, both in the United States and in several other rich countries. President Clinton, who had followed the first Bush administration in 1992 would be able to make some corrections to the part of the welfare system that had survived in the United States. He would add a requirement to search for work.

One important trend, that in time might lead to economic problems, was the beginning of increasing public and private borrowing in several countries, that would lead to large increases in public debts. This trend would become particularly marked in the new century.

Free trade and globalized policies became important, both in the exchange of goods and services, and in financial activities. The belief, strongly supported by many economists, was that a more open world would promote more *global* efficiency, more global growth, and more general welfare for the populations of the participating countries. There would be no expected losers in this globalizing movement toward efficiency, only winners. Among the many strong defenders of globalization there was, especially, Bhagwati (2004). However, some economists, including Stiglitz (2003), would express some concerns.

The cheaper, imported goods benefited the countries' consumers, and the new freedom to import cheaper inputs for their products also benefited many enterprises, by reducing their need to keep high inventories for some inputs. Supply shocks, that could damage some local economies, were not anticipated in these pro-trade policies and integrating world. "Just in time" systems of inventories were adopted by many enterprises. The assumption was that the mobility and the supply elasticity offered by many potential suppliers in a free, global market, allowed the enterprises to reduce their inventories and, thus, their costs. Potential supply shocks, that this policy might create, were generally ignored. These shocks would be important in 2020–2022, due to several developments, including the impact of the COVID-19 pandemic, the war in Ukraine, the growing competition between the United States and China, and the growing specialization of some new important products that only a few countries and enterprises could produce.

As for the US workers who might lose their jobs, due to the competition coming from the cheaper, imported products, they were expected to be able to move, smoothly and effortlessly, from their declining industries, and from their geographical areas, to the new, growing industries and areas, within their own countries. In the United States, Silicon Valley in California would become an attractive area for individuals with special abilities. Some Americans might even get better jobs abroad, as some foreigners had been getting good jobs in the United States. Some of the latter would even become very rich. Therefore, the loss of jobs for some workers was generally not seen as being a significant problem or one that merited much attention.

It was recognized that some of the workers who had been operating in the losing industrial sectors, sectors that were moving to lower costs countries, (such as China, India, Vietnam, Bangladesh), would lose their jobs, and many did, especially in the industrial sectors for which much production moved abroad. Many of these workers would discover that the mobility within the United States was often more limited than economists had assumed. Transition costs (both financial and psychological) were often high, and inadequate skills regarding the new jobs, and other factors, limited the moves for many. For some of those who lost their industrial jobs the alternatives were often low paying jobs.

Many workers got stuck in economically declining regions or industries, and there were no government programs ready to help them, in the new, pro-market environment created in those years. As is often the case in economics, what was thought to be theoretically right by economic theorists, proved to be partly wrong, or difficult in the real world.

Many economists had generally assumed the existence of a lot of mobility within countries' economies, and especially in one with a common language, such as the United States. Therefore, more dynamic and more flexible markets would make it easy, for workers who lost their jobs in a specific region or industry, to quickly move to other regions and to other jobs, that were being created within their own countries. Unfortunately, countries have continued to have less domestic flexibility and mobility than assumed. Therefore, many workers, who previously had had good jobs within their old communities, say Detroit, found themselves out of work, and with skills that were no longer in demand.

Because of family circumstances, some of these workers were also less willing or less able to leave the communities where they had lived. Attachment to their communities and to their old skills made them reluctant or unable to abandon the places where they had lived, and to move to places where other jobs, which were often less well-paying, or required different skills might be available, in the absence of government programs to assist them. The stronger had been the sense of community in the areas where they had lived, the harder it was to abandon them.

The increasingly libertarian economic thinking in those years discouraged governments from assisting workers in these moves and led to some problems. What was wrong was not the policy toward globalization and freer trade, but the way in which that policy was carried out, which ignored equity aspects. The net result would be that, over the longer run, globalization would acquire a less good reputation with the general public and there would be increasingly powerful forces leading to fragmentation, and to arguments in favor of more autarchic policies and the use of new restrictions. In the most recent years, some of these autarchic policies have created frictions between the Biden Administration and the European Union.

Supply shocks have become more intense in recent years, stimulated by the pandemic, the war in Ukraine, and the growing competition with China, which had become an increasing political competitor and a political challenger for the United States.

The financial market had also been liberalized and had become increasingly globalized after 1986. It was believed that a flexible financial market would help to spread risks and to grease the economic mechanism, helping the economies to promote higher economic growth. It might have done so, but at the cost of more potential future instability.

Alan Greenspan, a convinced libertarian, would become a strong proponent of financial liberalization from his influential position as the head of the US Federal Reserve Bank and would push for these policies. Banks and other financial institutions would become larger (see Greenspan, 2007; Shiller, 2012). The size of the financial market grew quickly and substantially in the decades that followed, attracting to it huge profits and many able individuals from other industries. For a while this promoted growth, until clouds started appearing.

The size of banks became much larger and their operations increasingly complex, raising questions as to whether they were becoming "too large to run and too big to fail." Before the Financial Crisis of 2007–2008, the size of the banks and their complexity had led some experts to question whether the banks might not in fact have become too large to be successfully managed. Linda Blair (2012), the former Chair of the Federal Deposit Insurance Corporation, had asked: "Are these financial institutions too big and too complex for anybody to manage?"

These institutions had in fact become "too big to fail." This meant that in case of their failure only the government (that is taxpayers' money) could rescue them. The government and the market were becoming increasingly mixed in many operations, and not necessarily because of the increasing role of the government in promoting equity and in regulating. As Paul Volcker would comment "I could give you stories all day about lobbyists making things more complex," including in the interpretations of his "Volcker rule," in the spirit of the old Glass Steagall law, the law that had separated commercial from investment banking.

This raised the question of whether new institutions and new laws were needed to protect the government from the pressures on it and from the distortions of needed government policies (including in public investments) by vested interests that tended to lead to a larger government in a presumably capitalist economy , one increasingly controlled by those with great financial means.

An interesting case was that of very rich individuals who created trusts and charitable institutions to promote social goals that they liked, as did Bill Gates and others, and as had been done a century earlier by Carnegie, Rockefeller, and others. These individuals got tax reductions for their giving, thus reducing the official tax level, while, to some extent, with their choices of charities or activities to support, they replaced the choices that the citizens would have made through the general budget. This, in some way, may have made the process less democratic in spite of the original merit of the decisions.

15

The Growing Importance of Monetary Policy

In those years, monetary policy came to be considered less limiting of the economic freedom of individuals than fiscal policy, and more effective. "Rational expectations theories" had raised questions about the efficacy of Keynesian countercyclical policy, in a world where the actions of "fully rational" agents would anticipate future policy actions neutralizing them. Thus, the importance of monetary action grew while that of fiscal action fell in the 1980s and later years.

Monetary policy became increasingly accommodating, allowing governments, to some extent, to replace tax revenue with public debt, in the financing of their public spending. "Maestros," such as Alan Greenspan, became popular. They were believed to know how to lead the orchestra that would promote a new great "moderation" in policy, one that would lead to greater prosperity, without major bumps (see Woodward, 2000). That moderation was increasingly associated with low Federal funds. Real interest rates were reduced to zero or even to negative values in many years.

A global market (both real and financial) and many internationally linked economic activities were created, and several countries and economic areas became integral parts of global activities and came to depend on inputs that came mainly from some countries or even from some areas within countries. Under normal circumstances, these links reduced the costs of production and the prices of many imported products. This helped consumers, in the importing countries, and producers and workers, in the exporting ones.

In an *efficient* market without random shocks, the global links would reduce the need by enterprises to keep large inventories, because the needed inventories would be assumed to be always available, when needed. Keeping inventories is expansive. However, cost saving, "just in time" inventory techniques inevitably expose the economies of countries to unexpected shocks and may contribute to shortages, to delays, and to increases in prices. This happened in 2020–2022, with the coming of the COVID-19 pandemic (see Tanzi, 2022). The unexpected Ukraine war, in 2022, would add to the already precarious situation. Also, as we shall see, technological developments were increasing the need for particular outputs, such as semiconductors and "rare earths" that were available in only a few places.

These in part *unexpected* events created supply disruptions which led to increases in the prices of some important inputs, such as petroleum, gas, grain, computer chips, rare metals, and others, the production of which was concentrated in specific countries. This made it difficult for some enterprises, such as car manufacturers and others, to maintain their production levels to meet demand and, for some families, to buy some needed products. To make matters worse, several countries had sharply increased public spending to fight the impact of the pandemic, leading to a rapid increase in inflation in many countries.

In this new, globalized and open world, the nationality of markets had been expected to play less of a role than in earlier times. But economic decisions still depended on *national* policies, and national policies require cooperation among countries' policies, when "public goods" become global, and when there are global "public bads" to deal with, such as pandemics and global warming. When such cooperation is missing, major problems may arise, and they arise more in a world that has become globalized. Unfortunately, at times, the real-world behaves differently from the way that the economic theories have suggested. The real world has the bad habit of presenting countries with unpleasant and unexpected surprises. This happens especially when the *political* objectives of different countries diverge, and when *politics* become the driver of economics rather than the other way around.

One undeniably good outcome of the globalization was that the income distribution for *the whole world population* became more equal over the years, because some previously very poor but very large countries, especially China and India, grew at much faster paces than the rich countries, due to the beneficial, medium-run effect of globalization on their economies. This reduced the differences in per capita income among countries.

A less positive outcome was that the income distribution *within many countries*, including China, India, the United States, the United Kingdom, and others became more unequal, and some categories of workers within advanced countries lost their good jobs and were left behind (see Milanovic, 2016). Globalization played a role in these changes, a role that was aggravated by the market fundamentalist policies of the 1980s and later.

With the passing of time the Gini coefficients became progressively higher in several countries, especially in the United States, and they started to raise pertinent questions about the process of globalization and the fairness of the current economic policies. For an early example, see Krugman (1994). During the recent pandemic years, popular reactions became less favorable toward the policies that had been adopted in recent decades, including the opening of markets. The risk of returning to autarkic or isolationist policies had recently increased.

In the years of market fundamentalism, the 1980s and 1990s, public spending generally resisted attempts by governments to reduce it, even though it did not continue to grow as fast as it had done in the decades when welfare states had been created. The conservative governments discovered that, politically, it was far easier to cut tax rates than to reduce public spending.

After the Great Recession of 2008–2010 and especially during the pandemic of 2020–2022, public spending increased sharply, to deal with the negative shocks on employment created by the financial crisis and, later, by the pandemic, even though the pandemic had decreased the supply more than the demand, so that higher spending was likely to lead to inflation. Public spending was financed by public borrowing made easier by the policies that the central banks had been promoting, including low rates and later "quantitative easing." The Federal Reserve in the United States would end up owing a large share of the US Federal debt, and the ECB a large share of the European public debt. Public debt grew at the fastest rate between the Great Recession and the pandemic years. It is expected to remain high and to continue to grow in future years in many countries including the United States. It is also likely to become more costly to service than it had been in the recent past.

Global public debt reached 91 percent of global GDP by 2022 and much higher levels in several countries, including Japan, Greece, Lebanon, and Italy. The world was literally drowning in public debt, and many countries were likely to face great difficulties in servicing it in future years, given the recent increases in the interest rates and the likely low growth of many economies (see the *IMF Fiscal Monitor* of October 2022).

In recent decades there has been a gradual but almost continuous increase in public debt in most countries. This increase had been facilitated and financed by the easy monetary policies that had been followed by the central banks. This had reduced the cost of borrowing to governments, making debt accumulation a politically preferable policy to that of raising taxes or cutting spending.

Some novel and at times difficult to accept economic theories, by Olivier Blanchard of MIT and others, had contributed to the above trend. The writings of Krugman, Stiglitz, Bernanke, and others had also directly or indirectly promoted public spending, during and after the Great Recession, when governments had been strongly urged to resist "austerity" policies and to maintain, or increase, public spending. That advice might have been reasonable at the time, to prevent the rise of unemployment, but it would lead to increasing worries in later years on how to service the public debt.

Those worries would become more intense when high inflation and higher interest rates returned in 2022, after the large recent fiscal deficits during the pandemic. Sustainability questions about the future are now being raised with more frequency than they had in past years.

In the United States, current projections for the Federal Government, based on unchanged current policies, made by the Congressional Budget Office, have indicated that the share of Federal debt into GDP will continue to rise and reach a record 110 percent in 2032, and much higher levels in later years. To this, one should add the debt of local governments (both actual and contingent) and the needs of public programs such as Social Security and Medicare and Medicaid, to get a more complete and increasingly worrisome picture of likely future difficulties.

Market fundamentalism had led to a shift from the active, Keynesian use of fiscal policy to the less intrusive monetary policy, that had been expected to promote full employment and growth, without creating inflation or major distortions in the allocation of resources. The governments had been given an instrument, cheap public debt, that politically seemed too good not to use.

Monetary policy was increasingly used to control and promote economic activity and to eliminate economic cycles. Its use had reduced the role that fiscal policy had played during the years of the Keynesian

Revolution in the afterwar decades. For a while, especially in the 1990s and the first half of the 2000s, this change seemed to work, leading some economists to believe that it might work forever.

The decade of the 1990s, which had made great use of monetary policy and limited use of fiscal policy, would be considered a period of "great moderation." It generated relatively good growth and gains in the stock market, and it was a period when the work of the market and the intervention of the government seemed to have achieved some desired harmony. Surveys in those years indicated that trust in government significantly increased in 1995–2000, as it had around 1965, around a different view. In his second term, the Clinton Administration would experience four years of Federal budget surpluses.

The policy changes in those years had generally been seen to be in the right direction, and the then chair of the US Federal Reserve System, Alan Greenspan, had earned the reputation of "maestro," for the firm and steady hand with which he had been guiding US monetary policy.

Globalization and the free trade that it had promoted, helped by the high saving rates of some fast-growing countries (especially China and other Asian countries) that invested part of their savings in the US dollar, as the world reserve currency, had helped contain the price increases that the financing of the public debt and the easy monetary policies might have caused in some of those years. Thus, foreign countries contributed to the financing of the US public debt and to keep the real interest rate and the rate of inflation low until 2022.

At the very beginning of the twenty-first century there had been a view (or a worry on the part of some) that US public debt might just vanish as a consequence of the budget surpluses that were reducing public debt. This would leave pension funds without any safe assets to buy, and the financial market without any available interest rate as a reference rate for safe investments. But the situation would soon change and fiscal deficits would return.

Until the year 2022, when inflation came roaring back like a tsunami and raised difficult questions for central banks on how to respond to it, some economists dismissed the danger of public debt, arguing that, in the long-term, the rate of growth of economies is generally higher than the cost of the debt. Therefore, the problem caused by the high public debt automatically solves itself, for countries that borrow in their own currency, as it had done after the Second World War for the United States.

Experiences of countries where this had not been the case were generally ignored or dismissed as irrelevant by the United States.

The return of high inflation worldwide was a wake-up call and it brought back the fear that the world might be again facing a period of stagflation in future years, as it did in the 1970s and the early 1980s. In the second half of 2022 this led to sharp falls in asset prices. Once again, the historical cycles had reminded us of their existence.

The next few years are likely to be interesting ones from an economic point of view. They will test recent economic thinking about debt and monetary policy and, possibly, in the process, also challenge the reputation of some economists. They may also reveal the existence of hidden debts, debts that tend to remain hidden in good times, but emerge in bad times and create difficulties for some financially exposed financial enterprises.

Today, there seems to be more uncertainty about what future policies will be or should be than the author of this book recalls there ever has been during his professional life, which has stretched for six decades. It is easy to anticipate the difficulties that will be faced, or are being faced, by highly leveraged financial institutions in the future months or years, and the pressures that may be created on governments to help those institutions, especially if they are too large to fail, as happened in 2008–2009. This will happen at a time when the governments will themselves be facing financial difficulties.

16

Equity Aspects of Market Fundamentalism

The coming of market fundamentalism in the late 1970s and 1980s represented not only a technical change in the use of economic policies, aimed at promoting some economic objectives better than in the past, but it also promoted a kind of profound ethical and even cultural revolution that, in the long-term, may have been more important than were the narrow, technical changes in the economic policies. This chapter will focus on distributional or equity aspects of market fundamentalism and, more directly, on cultural aspects.

The economic results that were generated by the work of the presumably freer market, in terms of income generation and income distribution, and in terms of the assignment of social values to the results of economic activities acquired in those years almost ethical justifications, given the cultural environment created. Those new values inevitably influenced relations among people and especially between income classes. See, especially, Sandel (2012) for calling particular attention to this aspect. It became more pleasant to be rich and easier to be greedy and to openly enjoy your wealth. High incomes and wealth came to be associated with hard work, more risk taking, more talent, and generally a more admiring personality. Wealth no longer needed to be hidden or justified by those who had it. They could flaunt it, as many rich individuals started to do in those years, and enjoy it to the fullest.

Being greedy was no longer seen as a negative trait, as it had been seen in the past. For some, it even became a virtue, because it could contribute to more productivity and to more national output, which were the important indices of performance and of society's wellbeing. Being greedy was accompanied by the strong desire to acquire more wealth, that could contribute to a higher output, that was an important social objective. On the contrary, being poor acquired, again, the connotation of being lazy, not daring, and of wanting to live at other people's expenses.

Altruism and philanthropy were no longer necessarily seen as virtues, as they had been seen by Catholic socialism and by many in the past (see Vickrey, 1962; Head, 1974, pp. 235–237). In the view of some individuals, they became potentially damaging traits, within the context of a free market economy, because they could lead to slower economic growth at a time when, as mentioned, growth had been elevated to be the main index of economic and social performance.

The scope of the market was expanded, by conservative economists such as Gary Becker and others, and came to encroach on, or to replace, some long-held traditional values, values that had been based on long-established community norms and not on market results. This had included the moral obligation of helping those in need. In the past, those traditional values had provided some useful glue for the communities. Many came to believe that market outcomes could not fail and were always right if they respected some agreed legitimate and shared rules. Therefore, whatever the market outcomes, the results should not be challenged once the market had determined them.

For example, a market for human organs was advocated in which those with higher incomes would naturally be able to outbid those with lower incomes for organs that could be transplanted, such as kidneys, hearts, and others. Blood sales, as distinguished from blood donations, were encouraged, and poor people (such as, at one time, the inhabitants of Haiti) were offered money to encourage them to sell their blood for use by those in the United States who could afford to pay for it. Why not have a global market for blood, rather than the Red Cross asking for blood donations?

Volunteer armies were advocated to fight wars, thus allowing rich kids to avoid serving in the army, or dying in wars, and many consultants were hired in what were de facto military operations, as they would be in the Iraq War. Private health services were encouraged and private schools, along with vouchers for selected public schools, were strongly recommended. Vouchers even influenced the school systems of countries, such as Sweden and some others, which had been less affected by the ideology of market fundamentalism.

The value of a human life was made to depend on the expected future earning power of individuals, making the lives of rich people more valuable than those of poor people. Damaging environmental garbage (such as used plastic and residues of dangerous chemicals) could be exported and sold to poor countries, as a World Bank document had advocated to do in those years, and as it was increasingly done in future years.

The view that the market was always right increasingly came to justify the asking for and the giving of very high compensation packages for some individuals (CEOs and other managers in general, and other individuals in particular activities), at a time when the marginal tax rates on high incomes were being sharply reduced. This combination would lead to enormous increases in the after-tax incomes of highly paid individuals and to income distributions that would become progressively less equal.

The differences between the incomes of the managers and those of the workers earning average, or minimum, wages grew and it became very large. Minimum wages continued to be criticized by economists, because they were supposed to create labor market rigidities, and lead to too high wages for some workers, thus reducing employment and company profits. The implication was that minimum wages ought to be lower, or, better, that they should not exist, so that the free market would determine wages at all levels. Income differences became as large as they had been at the end of the nineteenth century, when societies had been less democratic and when the tax systems and the public spending programs had not been helping in reducing the huge income differences, and many enterprises were then unregulated monopolies.

In the 1980s and later years, a period of privatization followed in many countries and in many areas, with privatization of public pensions, some schools, some jails, large infrastructures, fighting wars, dealing with some externalities, and even in the resolutions of some disputes between employees and enterprises (which came to be subjected to obligatory *private* arbitration).

It seemed that the free market could do everything better than the government, so that it could replace much of what governments had been doing. Some economists even started asking whether "Government by the Market" was not a realistic possibility (see Self, 1993). Some privately-run new towns were created in parts of the United States (as was Reston, in Virginia, near Washington DC) and some groups isolated themselves in closed, or gated and guarded, communities, for which they could set *private* and *shared* rules for small groups.

All the above were moves away from the spirit of large communities and of widely shared behavior, and in favor of free markets and "private clubs." These developments stressed *differences* between groups of people, and not *similarities* among the members of large communities. These attitudes could not fail to lead to less community spirit and to more individualistic behavior, in the years that followed.

Important changes in the tax systems (beside the dramatic reductions in the marginal tax rates) were introduced, such as changes in the "architecture" of the income tax, that gave preferential treatment to incomes from capital sources and reclassified some incomes as "low-taxed capital gains," (such as "carried trade" and compensations of managers received in shares), thus lowering the tax burdens on the high-income recipients. Depreciation allowances for enterprises were made more generous.

The view was that incomes from capital deserved better tax treatment than incomes from wages: because capital was more mobile; to encourage incentives to invest; and it was necessary to provide incentives to high-income individuals, because these were the individuals who generated economic growth. Past tax principles, such as rates based on ability to pay, were progressively abandoned and there were calls for low tax rates and for flat taxes. Taxation became increasingly complex and less progressive (see Messere, 1993; and articles in Shome, 2022).

In important sectors (such as the financial market, the labor market, and the corporate sector) regulations were sharply reduced and financial and corporate operators acquired much freer hands in promoting the expansion of a "shadow banking system," a system that became progressively more important and that helped finance increasingly complex and risky loans.

Not surprisingly, with the passing of time, the number of individuals engaged in these financial operators increased significantly. The shadow banking system also became a factor in facilitating the growth of both public and private debt. As we shall see in Chapter 17, some industrial enterprises (such as General Electric), increasingly became, de facto, unregulated banks, in their total activities, that also became more and more globalized.

Many large loans were made, increasingly financed not by individuals' savings but by borrowing. They, essentially, became bets on future outcomes and not genuine investments in real economic activities, financed by genuine savings. Their contribution to the welfare of society became increasingly questionable but was strongly defended, while their contribution to large potential future risks tended to be ignored (see Mitchell, 2007).

Some of these risks would materialize in later years when they would force governments to intervene on a very large scale and at taxpayers' expenses, as the US Federal government was forced to do in 2008–2009 to save some large banks from bankruptcy and the financial system from collapse (see Morris 2008; Blinder, 2013; Glantz, 2019; Bernanke, 2022).

Similar worries reappeared in 2022, at a time when: governments were already overburdened by very large debts; the current high inflation was requiring large increases in interest rates; and the stakes seemed to be higher, because of the high existing debts. It was not difficult to anticipate a bumpy future ride in different economies and, possibly, future stagnation, recessions, or more dangerous developments.

In some areas, the financial market was no longer financing genuine *investments*, that is additions to real, productive capital that could be expected to generate future growth, but it was largely financing gambling operations of questionable value to the economy. Some economists continued to believe that these gambling operations somehow contributed to a better allocation of the available resources.

The market for "derivatives," accompanied by "credit swaps" and by other complex financial instruments, grew enormously and so did "leveraged loans," creating high potential risks and future instability in the economy (see Leonard, 2022). In the short-term, the market could create huge gains for some lucky operators, thus further contributing to income inequality. Some of these operators had been able to experience billion dollar gains or losses in single days.

The share of total profits received by the financial market grew significantly after the 1980s. From time to time, some financial difficulties, including the failures of Long-Term Capital Management, Enron, and the dot-com collapse at the end of the century would happen, but they did not much change the social environment. Trust in the market was not shaken, however, hose difficulties would be followed by the much more serious "Financial Market Crisis" of 2007–2008, which would lead to the collapse of some very large banks and cause the "Great Recession" of 2009–2010. That crises would begin to change the environment, and the market fundamentalist policies would come under sharp attacks from some quarters and major economists. The honeymoon with market fundamentalism was over.

In 2022, new, major difficulties would appear, especially those connected with rapid increases in prices. They would force the Federal Reserve and other Central Banks to change the relaxed monetary policies that they had been following for a long time and to begin to increase interest rates, with commitments to keep increasing them until inflation was brought under control.

It became increasingly difficult to predict the longer run effects of the developments of 2008–2010, especially on highly leveraged institutions and on highly indebted governments. As could be expected the stock market and the housing market reacted strongly, and some investment banks faced major short-term losses.

The separation between commercial and investment banking, which had been introduced in the 1930s, was eliminated in the 1980s to give more flexibility to financial operators and more freedom to the market. This elimination had allowed financial institutions to increase their risks and to spread them more widely among their lending activities. For example, the securitization of home mortgages, that had financed the construction and the purchase of new houses, had reduced the standards that had previously been applied in the past in giving such loans. Increasingly, people with "no incomes and no jobs" had managed to get many of these loans and to buy houses that they should not have been able to afford. In turn, these mortgages had been securitized in new instruments and had been resold, in packages in which the risks of the individual loans had been hidden, having been spread. The risks would be passed on to unwary investors, often pension funds, in their securitized versions. Irrationality in human behavior, hidden risks, and market exuberance would be discovered to have been common occurrences.

The complexity of new financial instruments had facilitated these maneuvers, because those who had bought the securitized instruments often did not fully understand them and the risks that they were taking when they bought them. What could have been less risky that a loan backed by *many* mortgages, all in turn backed by new houses, the value of which had been going up in past years, and was expected to continue to go up? Those who had bought many of these new houses had in turn bought them under the expectation that the prices of the houses would keep going up, as they had done in previous years. Many had bought the houses not to live in them but to make money on their future sales. Market exuberance, some irrationality, and risk shifting had combined to create potential future difficulties.

The share of finance in total corporate profits in the United States increased, from around 15 percent in the early 1970s to over 40 percent in the early years of the new century. Debt kept rising, and not only in the public sector. The share of private debts into GDPs also reached high, historical levels in the most recent years, raising pressing questions as to what would happen when interest rates had to increase enough to fight high and sustained inflation, as they had done in 1982, and as they were doing in 2022 and early 2023, when the Federal Reserve and other central banks had been forced to take actions to fight the suddenly strong inflationary pressures.

While the initial stock market "reaction" has been predictable to these actions, that of the real economy has been less predictable. As of early 2023, employment and growth have not been much affected.

During the years of market fundamentalism, the labor unions lost many of their members and much of the powers that they had had in the previous decades, while the managers of the financial institutions and economic enterprises acquired far more power than they had in earlier decades. The power of the new managers within their enterprises approached that which the owners of enterprises had a century earlier, especially when the current managers could appoint members of their boards, and many managers have been fully using that power.

Obviously, relations between workers and managers have deteriorated in recent decades and continued to deteriorate in recent times. In various enterprises, such as Amazon, air lines, hospitals, etc., labor unions have started to give some sign of waking up, and strikes might again become realistic possibilities in the future of some sectors. However, union membership has remained low for the time being and the structure of the labor market makes it less easy to unionization now. However, in some sectors we are likely to have different relations between employers and employees in future years.

The managers of enterprises have continued to receive high compensations, presumably justified by their "exceptionally rare talent" and their "extremely hard work." The compensations have included huge bonuses and free corporate shares which can be worth millions of dollars, beside other perks, such as retirement packages, which became not only large but less transparent parts of their total compensation.

At times, those total compensations have become so large as to have been unthinkable, or even absurd, in the decades after the Second World War or, even today, in some other advanced countries. In recent years the private perks of managers have even included the availability of private jets, memberships in expensive clubs, and others.

Clearly, managers have begun to consider themselves members of a new privileged class. For example, in the latest Davos Meeting in Switzerland, more than a thousand participants arrived in private jets. These high compensations have contributed a great deal to make the income distributions of the United States, the United Kingdom and other countries in recent decades increasingly uneven and the compensations have been structured to reduce, as much as possible, the tax liabilities on them.

In May 2022, in a rare action, the shareholders of J. P. Morgan voted against a proposal to give its Chief Executive a bonus which was potentially worth $50 million, this at a time when dark clouds had appeared on the horizon. The shareholders had considered the size of that award a bit too much. By that time that CEO's past compensations had already made him a billionaire, according to Forbes calculations (see article in *The Financial Times*, May 18, 2022, p. 1). Also, some shareholders of Tesla sued over Elon Musk's compensation of $50 billion from Tesla in 2017. At that time Musk had been running four different and unrelated companies.

These enormous compensation packages had been made possible in part by keeping the wages of the mostly nonunionized and powerless workers as low as possible, and in part by shifting some production activities to countries with even lower wages; or engaging in more market manipulations to increase the value of the shares in the short-term. Or, in the case of financial enterprises, by taking larger risks with their operations.

The large compensations were justified by the argument that the managers offered exceptional talent and, through that talent and their hard work, contributed a lot to the profits of the corporations and the general economic welfare. It was maintained that their compensations were fully merited and were determined exclusively by the free market forces. Connections and the power of elite networks presumably played no roles in these decisions. For the role that elites can play in the distribution of income and power, see Vukovic's interesting work, *Elite Networks: The Political Economy of Inequality* (unpublished).

Accounting tricks would often be used by the managers of corporations to inflate the short-term profits of their companies, which were the profits that determined large parts of their compensation packages. The companies have been reluctant to reveal the full details of the compensation packages of their managers.

As mentioned, the power of the workers and of the labor unions greatly declined after the 1970s. In the United States, the share of workers who had belonged to unions fell from more than 30 percent in the 1960s to about 10 percent in recent years, but their power had fallen even more. There was an equivalent fall in the United Kingdom. Thatcher and Reagan had played important roles in those declines. Changes in the structures of the economies had done the rest.

The share of labor income in total income fell, in the United States, from about 67 percent in 1967 to about 56 percent after the Great Recession.

Many workers now work at minimum wages, especially in some states, such as Texas, and the minimum wages that they receive have continued to be criticized by some economists because, in their view, they create rigidity in the labor market. Presumably, in the absence of statutory minimum wages, many workers would get even lower real wages, to make the market more flexible and efficient, and to allow even higher compensations to the highly paid managers or higher profits to the shareholders (see Yu, Markad, and Shunko, 2022).

Available estimates indicate that normal, dependent workers benefited little, or not at all, from the globalization, the deregulation, and the more libertarian policies of recent decades. For many, their average tax levels and their real wages did not change much over several decades. Many of those who, in the decades before the 1980s, had been involved in the production of locally made, industrial goods, goods that in later decades were increasingly imported from low wages countries, lost their jobs, and experienced real and often permanent income losses or reductions.

In the absence of redistributive policies, which continued to be opposed by market fundamentalists, this, again, tended to make the income distributions less equal than they had been in the post-war decades, while the share of total profits in national income rose and the share of income going to the top few percentages in the income distributions, especially the top 1 percent, also increased sharply.

The supporters of the supply-side revolution had expected great benefits in terms of output growth from that revolution, and they had sold it to the public with the promise that it would generate miracles in terms of economic efficiency and economic growth and gains in the real wages of most workers, due to more investment and higher productivity. These expectations had largely not been achieved.

By the late 1970s the small-government and more market ideology had acquired many followers. The policy changes that it advocated had not been expected to make the income distributions more unequal. "Trickle down effects" from the libertarian policies had been promised and had been expected to benefit everyone, not just a few. Unfortunately, growth did not pick up as much as it had been expected and, perhaps much more importantly, the growth that occurred did not benefit a large share of the working population as had been expected. It did, in fact, benefit relatively few individuals in higher income categories. Many workers were left worse off, when they lost their previously held and better-paying jobs, as happened in Detroit and in other places in the United States, parts of the United Kingdom, and other advanced economies (see Vance, 2016; Hill, 2021). Remarkably, even when in the more recent years the unemployment rates were very low, the income of average workers did not improve.

The income and wealth distributions of several countries, as measured by the Gini coefficient, and especially those of the United States and United Kingdom, became much less equal in the 1980s and later years than they had been in the 1960s and 1970s. Furthermore, as extensive empirical research by Raj Chetty et al. (2014) has shown, social mobility fell over the years so that the chance that the children of poorer workers would have higher incomes than their parents fell significantly, even in the presence of growth. It fell from more than 90 percent in the 1940s to 50 percent in the 1980s and to lower levels in later years. Social mobility was significantly influenced by various characteristics of the families and by the locations where children were brought up. These factors included education of parents, health, attitudes, etc.

The power of the market alone could not remove some of the existing constraints on social mobility and perhaps neither could the traditional social welfare programs that simply provided some temporary extra income to the poor, without much changing that environment, as Chetty and colleagues pointed out in their work. The government had to play a role with efficient and well-focused programs sustained over many years. It might have to be a role different from the traditional one concentrated on just increasing the income of the current poor, with less attention to factors that influence social mobility. Low income is only one of the characteristics of the poor, with poor health and lack of motivation often being equally important. For example, educated individuals often end up marrying educated individuals, thus helping to perpetuate the existing income and class distributions.

In the United States, the Gini coefficients for income rose by about ten points, from the 1970s until current years, or from less than .40 in the 1970s to .49 in 2021, according to the US Census Bureau. That was a very large increase. The Gini started to increase in the early 1980s and the increase accelerated in the 1990s. But social mobility had started to fall even earlier. Taxes reduced inequality by about 13 percent, not a large change.

In the United Kingdom the Gini was about .25 in 1978 and rose to .38 by 2007. It then fell to .34 by 2021. In both these countries the impact of the fundamentalist policies introduced on income distribution, by Thatcher and Reagan, was unmistakable.

In 1980, in the United States, the top 1 percent of the income distribution had received about 10 percent of the total income. Forty years later the share had exceeded 20 percent. Income gains had been widely shared until the 1970s. After that period much of the income gains went to the top 1 or 5 percent (see Piketty, Saez, and Zucman, 2018).

Much of the growth in income that took place in the 1980s and later benefited a relatively small share of the population, mostly those in the top percentages of the income distribution and, even more, a few hundred billionaires, some of whom became as rich as had been the "robber barons" at the end of the nineteenth century. Inevitably individuals in nonwhite ethnic groups were predominantly in the low-income percentages.

Perhaps it ought to be mentioned that some debate remains among economists on the accuracy of the available estimates on inequality. Some of the estimates of growing inequality have been challenged by conservatives (see, Burtless, 2014).

Not only has the *economic* power of the rich grown but also their *political* power , as could be expected in a "political market" where those who have more money can buy more *political* power by influencing votes, laws, and regulations in their favor. This more worrisome aspect will be discussed more fully in a later chapter. Some official policy changes have facilitated that change.

The expected "trickle down" or "levelling up" that was expected "to raise all boats" never materialized, and many boats remained permanently grounded. "Trickle down" did not raise the wages of most dependent workers. For many, the real wages remained broadly unchanged in real terms for four decades, and for some they even fell.

The share of total income and wealth received by the top 1 percent of the population, a share that had fallen from the 1930s until the mid-1970s, started increasing at a fast pace and, in the United States, reached the highest levels in 2021. Then the situation started to change, when the stock market suffered some losses, reducing the wealth of the rich and some of the wealth accumulated in the 401k accounts of the middle and higher classes.

Available reports have indicated that the compensations of managers in the United States continued to rise at least until Summer 2022, while those in the United Kingdom have been undergoing a difficult period in the most recent years.

17

Other Aspects of Market Fundamentalism

The supply-side revolution had come at a time when both the operations of the market and the activities of governments (including those in social programs and writing of laws and regulations) had become increasingly complex. The growing complexity and other changes (such as the digitized economy) had created new opportunities for clever, well-informed, and less scrupulous individuals, and for well-paid lobbyists who increasingly represented special interest groups and were financed by them, to exploit both some of the operations of the complex market and those of the governments. Some companies were created to gather information on the behavior and the preferences of citizens. That information was sold to lobbyists representing special interests and was used by the latter to better target their lobbying activities.

What could be called "termites" were being created in the market and, because of them, the market was becoming increasingly less "perfect" or less efficient, in spite of the deregulation movement that was going on (see, Tanzi, 2001, 2018a). Termites are small changes in rules that, often, go unobserved when made but can have major consequences, as have biological termites that, over long periods, can destroy large wooden structures.

The complexity was also affecting the democratic process because that process assumes, or must assume, that citizens vote for policies that they fully understand and can, thus, judge. When the policies become too complex, many citizens fail to understand what they are voting for, and tend to be more easily influenced by lobbyists, by publicity, and by "fake news." This can lead to unexpected election and other results, corrupting the democratic process.

This has been happening in recent years in some countries and, perhaps, in the United States more than others. Those who have more financial means to promote "fake news" inevitably acquire more market and more political power in these circumstances. This is the classic "golden rule." Those who have the gold end up making the rules

Technological and other developments, which were only partly connected with the undergoing policies, had also been creating opportunities for some clever and lucky individuals to increase their earnings. This was especially the case with the *digitation* of the economy, brought by the "second machine age." While the "first machine age," that had been an important part of the Industrial Revolution, had provided cheap energy to replace, or to add to, human muscles, the "second machine age" was bringing and adding to human brains. The new power could be directed toward good but also less good purposes (see Brynjolfsson and McAfee, 2014; Agrawal, Gans, and Goldfarb, 2018). For sure, it could not fail to have an impact on the income distribution by, at least initially, replacing low wage workers with robots in many basic tasks, as it has started to do.

These developments were making a few individuals rich, by extracting small gains from very large numbers of customers and by receiving large total payments that, de facto and increasingly, could be defined, at least in part, as "rents." Rents are defined as legal but *unearned* compensations, rather than *genuine and deserved* incomes. The increased wealth was giving these individuals more market and more political power.

The new economic, social, and technological environment had its origin in the recently changed policies but also in new technological developments which were only partly linked to those policies. It might have happened in any case but, perhaps, it would have happened at a slower pace and in a less dramatic fashion than it did.

In this new environment, an increasing number of knowledgeable observers started to define the capitalist system, as it was operating, as "crony" or "casino" capitalism (see Rajan, 2010; Sinn, 2010, and others). And some authors started talking about "market exuberance" and mistakes that investors often make because of irrational behavior, partly created by the exuberance.

This irrationality view challenged the traditional one, which had been strongly held by Chicago School economists and by Milton Friedman (1963) in particular, that individuals are rational and act rationally (see Shiller, 2000; Ariely, 2008; Smith, 2008). In recent experiments, Irrational behavior has turned out to be far more common than previously thought, thus challenging the assumption of rationality.

In many ways, the system that had been created during those years
started to resemble less and less the ideal system that had been visualized
and described by economists such as Hayek, Von Mises, Friedman, and
Stigler, and that was assumed to be still possible by libertarian and
conservative economists and by many conservative individuals.

Such a system might no longer be possible in the new world that had
come into existence, and more deregulation of the current system might
not be the answer, because those who would make the decisions might
also be affected by irrationality and the reduction in rules might encourage less honest behavior.

With the impact of new technological developments, with globalized
economic activities, and with the availability of enormous financial capital
concentrated in a few, private hands, the free market had changed in
important and unanticipated ways, and would continue to change. The
question has become whether a truly free market is still possible in a world
with a highly concentrated income distribution, as conservative economists continue to believe. The modern market has come to resemble less
and less the cozy and efficient local market described and idealized by
economists of the Austrian School and at the Chicago School and, in many
exchanges, it has been creating "lemons," using the colorful terminology
first used by George Akerlof (1970) in his famous article. It has also been
creating other distortions. "Lemons" are market exchanges in which the
symmetry that should exist in the information available to *both* sides of the
exchanges, and the equal freedom of action of the agents, may be missing.

The presence of "lemons" in market exchanges can originate from
several causes. That presence seems to have significantly increased in
recent decades, due to the increasing importance of services in the
exchanges and the expansion of the market in many other directions,
making the supposedly freer market of recent decades in some ways less
efficient, more prone to abuse, and less egalitarian than it had been in
the past.

Especially in some financial exchanges, the asymmetry created by the
complexity of the financial instruments prevented one side of the
exchange to fully understand what it was agreeing to, and financial
exchanges had increased enormously in recent decades. Just recall the
example of the sale of *secularized* mortgage loans to pension funds, in the
years before the Great Recession. The buyers of those instruments had no
understanding of the risks that the instruments carried, when they bought
them, and this was a free market transaction, and one even among
presumably knowledgeable parties.

An increasing share of the enormous exchanges that now take place daily in the market can no longer be assumed to be automatically welfare improving, as they had been assumed in the past, for what were thought to be well-behaved markets that exchanged known products among individuals who often knew one other. Because of increasing complexity and other factors, "termites" have frequently entered in many transactions, in both the operations within market, such as in the sale of goods, and in some of the exchanges between citizens and government, such as the payment of taxes or the interpretation of regulations (see Saez and Zucman, 2019).

The UN office on Drugs and Crime has reported that half a million Africans are now killed every year by the use of fake medicines. *The Economist* has reported that the real action in finance is now outside regulated banking. And a study by the United Nations University World Institute for Development Economic Research (UNU-Wider) has shown that close to a trillion dollars, or 40 percent of the profits of multinational enterprises had been shifted to tax havens in 2019, equivalent to 10 percent of corporate tax revenue. Like their biological counterparts, these various "termites" have been doing their damages slowly and often in the dark, thus defying easy observation.

The sectors of the economy in which asymmetry in information can easily exist have been growing as shares of total exchanges and of countries' GDPs. These sectors include finance, which has become very complex and very global; insurance, which has grown a lot, covering areas in which it is difficult to determine statistically the expected outcomes; and especially the private health sector.

In the United States, the private health industry has grown a lot over the years and has been accompanied by increasing complexity, abuse, and other problems. Just think of the bills that many patients receive after even short hospital stays, and the huge differences in the prices of the same drugs between the United States and other countries. The US health sector (that combines some public and some privately insured activities) has become very expensive, without showing good results in terms of life expectancy and good health for the whole population.

Some other services, such as house and car repairs; the provision of various tourist and legal services; the exchanges of services across frontiers; and educational services (just think of the Trump University that would teach individuals how to become millionaires!) have also been showing characteristics of "lemons" in the free market.

Educational services and health services have become very expensive and have led to enormous debts for students and patients who had borrowed to finance their studies, and for patients who underwent medical procedures, some of which might not have been needed, and that often turned out to be much more expensive and less beneficial than anticipated. Getting ill or getting better educated has, at times, become a direct way to going broke for many individuals.

As reported earlier in this chapter, "termites" have increasingly entered tax policies, and naturally they are playing a role in tax avoidance. Tax avoidance and tax evasion have become increasingly common, making the real tax system less fair and less productive in tax revenue than the statutory one might indicate. There are now very large corporations and even billionaires that pay taxes that are small shares of their real incomes, and that, in some cases, are smaller shares of the taxes paid by normal workers who receive low wages, as several recent estimates have shown.

Many modern products and services have become too complex for their value to be easily determined or understood by the normal citizens who buy them, and many products (including the growing share of "fake products" in the market) are no longer bought from nearby and known suppliers, as they had been in the distant past, when exchanges had been mostly among locals, and had been mostly confined between individuals who knew one another.

Many of the products or services consumed in the modern, globalized economies are now imported from faraway places and producers and are produced under unknown environmental and other conditions. Complexity has become a pervasive parameter in the lives of many citizens and deregulation has not removed and cannot remove it from their daily lives. It is likely that deregulation has increased complexity and abuses, as happened in the financial market.

The frequent asymmetries in exchanges have reduced or nullified many of the expected welfare gains that should come from market exchanges. *Ex ante*, it has become difficult, for an average person, to know precisely the real value of what that person is getting from an exchange, or from a contract, as many individuals discovered in the financial transactions (some global ones) that led to the "sub-prime crisis" of 2007–2008 (see Glantz, 2019) or to the earlier Enron crisis.

Often the terms of formal contracts are buried in pages of fine print, and the often-lengthy documents, which are rarely read, are written in "legalese," a language that only few insiders can fully understand.

The asymmetry in information has also worked its way into many operations of the public sector, including the new laws that have routinely become thousands of pages long and that, normally, are written by assistants to the legislators or to the policymakers, and are approved by legislators who, in many cases, have not read the full bills (see Tanzi, 2011). The drafting of the laws or regulations has often received some behind-the-scenes input from interested lobbies, representing those who will be most affected by them. Proximity between a lobbyist and representatives of the public sector generally plays a role in these contacts.

Termites (including the behind-the-scenes work of lobbies) can easily penetrate the writing of the laws and the regulations during their preparation, when they are being considered and are being written; and/or they can also change the interpretations of the laws and of the regulations during their use at later times.

The existing laws have grown in numbers in many countries (e.g., the United States and Italy) and there are now tens of thousands of them. They often leave scope for different interpretations, which are exploited by enterprises and their lobbies, that have more money, means, and direct interests in them and can spend more time on analyzing them.

These developments have created an almost impenetrable "legal jungle" for most citizens, a jungle that can easily be exploited and that is being increasingly exploited by special interest groups, who have the skills, time, manpower, and interest to penetrate them, as well as the deep pockets to finance the needed resources to do so.

The result has been a less transparent and more random form of "mercantilism" than the one that had existed during Adam Smith's times. Privileged, well-connected, and clever individuals have been the major beneficiaries of some of the governments' activities in recent decades. The losers have been normal workers and the general public. Much of the above occurred during the years of market fundamentalism.

Given all of this, to believe that a libertarian world, one without a government or with a very limited government role, would be an option that would make everyone free and prosperous, as some have continued to sustain, is just a summer dream. Of course, if the concept of sin, or that of crime, were eliminated citizens would all live in a world without official sins and crimes. But it might not be the ideal or dream world that libertarians continue to believe in.

18

Cultural Aspects of Market Fundamentalism

The intellectual and policy changes, that began in the late 1970s, could not have failed to also generate significant changes in relations among individuals and between economic classes, or in the general culture of countries. In this chapter we shall identify a few individuals who, directly or indirectly, may have been partly responsible for some of these cultural changes, or have contributed to them. However, it must be recognized and stressed that there were many other individuals and factors that also contributed to the changes.

Perhaps the first individual that should be mentioned ought to be Milton Friedman, who, in many of his pronouncements in those years and, especially, in an essay that he published in *New York Times Magazine*, on September 21, 1970, attracted a lot of attention at the time and continued to attract attention over many years. In that essay, written for the general readers of the *New York Times Magazine* and not just for economists; and written at a time when advanced economies had started to face strong head winds; and when there were increasing societal divisions, caused by the Vietnam War and by other factors (some of which had led to the events of 1968 in several countries), Friedman argued that "the social responsibility of business is to increase profits," period. Any other objective, such as maintaining workers happiness, contributing to a more equitable income distribution, or worrying about environmental degradation, would distract business leaders from that main objective, and in his view would end up being damaging and even dangerous for society. He argued that, in the longer term, that distraction would end up damaging both the economy and general welfare. In other words, community goals should simply be ignored by business leaders, if these goals existed, and only the interests of the shareholders of the enterprises should be promotes by the companies' managers. Friedman's plea had not been published in an economic journal, where only economists would see it, but in a publication widely read by the general public.

It is not difficult to see what such a position, maintained by a top economist, who, by that time, had become a very influential and widely followed public intellectual and media personality, could do to the relations between managers and workers in corporations, especially at a time when labor unions were still strong but had started to come under attack for their negative impact on productivity.

Many conservative economists and managers enthusiastically endorsed Friedman's advice, while members of the general public and most workers must have been shocked by Friedman's position. One of the consequences of following Friedman's advice was that squeezing workers' wages and pushing activities abroad started to be seen as good policies, if such actions could lead to higher short-term corporate profits, as they often could.

In future years the share of profits in national income would start going up, and that of wages would go down, with obvious effects on the income distribution. Other interventions by Friedman in those years went in the same libertarian direction. The cutting of taxes on profits would be a natural policy consequence.

While the influence of Friedman, important as it was, may have been largely intellectual, another individual who, in the 1980s and 1990s, would play a large and more direct role in the US corporate culture and in influencing the behavior of US managers was Jack Welsh who, in 1981, became the CEO of General Electric, which was then a large and historically important American corporation. In the years that followed, Welsh would come to be considered, by many, as "the greatest chief executive of all time" (see Gelles, 2022, p. 1).

There is little doubt that Welsh's influence on US corporate culture was direct and enormous. Some would remember him as an almost godlike figure, who, like the Pope, could not make mistakes (Ibid.). Welsh set the example of how managers should behave and how they should run their companies. The welfare of the workers would become totally irrelevant and the face of capitalism, or "the tide that would raise all boats", would change in a dramatic way. The "compassion" would simply disappear from the capitalistic system and the short-term pursuit of profits would reign supreme, as Friedman had suggested it should a decade earlier.

During Welsh's time, General Electric became the most valuable company in the world. In the process it also changed American corporate culture in important ways. He trained many individuals, who went on to run other corporations, expecting to make them as profitable as General Electric had become. They brought to their positions Welsh's management culture and style and created an elite network that would make that culture common and normal, at least in the United States and perhaps in some other Anglo-Saxon countries that were influenced by the US example. However, these individuals would not be able to achieve as good profit results in their companies as Welsh had achieved at General Electric. Welsh campaigned strongly against taxes and against government regulations that, in his view, reduced the CEOs' power and the profits of corporations.

When he retired from General Electric, in 2001, already a very rich man because of the annual compensations he had received from General Electric for two decades, he got a $417 million retirement package. That package helped set the stage for what CEOs would expect to receive when they retired, in later years, from other corporations, and such extraordinary retirement packages became common in the US corporate sector.

All the above was happening at a time when many workers were losing their defined benefit pensions and other benefits, and when they had seen little or no increases in their real wages for many years. Welsh's management style became legendary, for both its aggressiveness and its total lack of any empathy toward subordinates, and especially toward workers. Cost cutting at any cost, and to any extent possible, was the main tool that he employed. Any obstacle toward that objective and toward higher, short-term corporate profits, had to be removed, regardless of the human and social costs involved in doing so.

To achieve this objective, he introduced the system of annual firing of the presumably 10 percent less productive of the workforce at General Electric. Ten percent of the workers were fired every year without any regard for their wellbeing or for their family situations. This policy gave Welsh the nickname of "Neutron Jack," because, like neutron bombs are assumed to do, he destroyed workers but saved things and profits. The workers were considered robots, without feelings, and the government was discouraged from assisting them with welfare programs, because of the higher taxes that this assistance would require. Profits were good, taxes were definitely "socialist."

In the two decades that he spent managing GE, Welsh transformed that proud industrial company into a financial institution, one that increasingly used questionable accounting maneuvers, including mergers and acquisitions, both domestic and foreign, to achieve short-term profits. By the time he left General Electric, that company had become more a financial institution than the proud industrial company that it had been in the past.

The US Federal Trade Commission would later find several questionable practices in the actions that Welsh had taken in achieving the continuous high, short-term profits during his years (see Gelles, 2022). In November 2021 the enterprise announced that it would split into three separate enterprises.

Not surprising, in later years Welsh became a strong supporter of President Trump and of his policies. In his popular television program, *The Internist*, Trump would frequently use, with effect, a sentence that must have been inspired by, or borrowed from, Welsh: "you are fired!"

The above discussion has focused mainly on the direct relations, since the 1970s, between dependent workers and managers of enterprises. The workers were clearly the losers in those years, and the managers and the shareholders the winners, a change that significantly affected US income distribution. Those who had been *industrial* workers especially lost out when their union power was reduced and when many industrial activities moved to countries where wages were much lower and unions did not exist. Or they lost out when robots started taking away some of the workers' past functions. Today, a manager that reminds one of Welsh, and that occasionally behaves in a similar fashion, is Elon Mask.

Changes in the pension and in the health systems in those years reduced the connection, links, and loyalty that had existed between workers and the enterprises for which they had worked for much of their lives. Many workers not only lost their good jobs and decent incomes but also some of their dignity and self-respect. They no longer felt pride in working for their companies. Links between workers and the companies in which they worked became much more tenuous with obvious cultural implications.

Before closing this chapter, there is another individual that, perhaps, merits a mention, because of the impact that he had, not on economic relations but on cultural and political relations, at that and later times. That individual is Newt Gingrich. His impact was mainly and directly related to the political world.

During Reagan's Administration years, and during the administration of the first President Bush, personal relations between political opponents and parties had remained relatively cordial, even when political views had been widely divergent. During the early Clinton years those good relations had made it possible to bring some reforms to the existing welfare system. That cordial world would change and in a dramatic way in the following decade, with the coming of Newt Gingrich to the US Congress.

Gingrich brought to politics an adversarial style that was much rougher and that changed the political and cultural atmosphere. It was no longer sufficient to disagree with your political opponents and stress your disagreement and the reasons for it. You had to attack and humiliate them. This cultural change became the norm in the US political arena. It has survived and has become more intense in recent years, when politics has indeed become a very rough sport.

The individuals mentioned above have helped in changing, in dramatic ways, the cultural environment of the United States in recent decades. The change would manifest itself in many areas, including the way people dressed; the publicity shown in television programs, that not only changed from advertising soaps and cars, as in the 1960s and 1970s, to advertising mainly insurances and drugs, but also increasingly treating viewers as idiots. Dignified behavior was out, eccentric behavior was in.

Last names disappeared when one was contacted by perfect strangers, who addressed you by first name, as if you had known each other for a long time and regardless of age differences. This shift was symbolic of a change from an identification which reflected a small community (the family is a small community) to a first name that is strictly individual. These and others were indications of the cultural changes that had taken place between the 1970s and the new century. It should be stressed that not all the mentioned changes were generated by the few individuals mentioned in this chapter. They naturally reflected broader social developments.

19

Growing Conflict between Efficiency and Equity

During the 1980s and 1990s, marginal tax rates were dramatically reduced in the United States and other advanced countries, especially the rates on the highest incomes of individuals and those on capital incomes, including those on corporate profits. The declared goal of these reductions was to promote economic efficiency and faster economic growth. This was happening at a time when the incomes being received by a small share of individuals had started to rise rapidly, due to the new social and technological environment and the changing policies. The new environment would make relatively few individuals the major beneficiary of the tax reforms and of new policies.

For a variety of technological, economic, and policy reasons, in an increasing number of cases the incomes of some individuals and some enterprises were acquiring aspects that made them resemble more to classic "rents" than to fully earned and genuine "incomes" (see Tanzi, 2014b; 2018a, ch. 30). For more recent examples see Goodman (2022). Simply put, some individuals were benefiting from favorable situations not created by them. These situations especially included the free access to scientific discoveries and knowledge (especially in the biological and technological areas), that had become available in the decades after the Second World War.

These fundamental discoveries had been financed by public money. A few clever individuals were benefiting from them and also from recently-created technological platforms (such as television, the Internet, and GPS) that had become available because of government-financed research originally connected with military uses or with defense objectives, financed largely by military budgets.

The output of the basic research accumulated over many decades, especially in the cold war decades after the Second World War, made it possible for clever individuals to use the available scientific knowledge to develop new technologies and to benefit from them. To some extent these individuals were benefitting from "rents" and also from the lower, recently-legislated tax rates on high earnings. They were also benefitting from the globalization policies that had expanded the size of the potential users.

The fundamental knowledge, that was freely available to anyone capable of using it, and the new platforms that had been created in the recent past for transmitting information, could be used by clever individuals to generate new products and especially services that could be sold to a worldwide audience. At least initially, those who provided them could also benefit from the protections offered by patent laws or by other "intellectual property" protection rules.

The government had, indirectly, *subsidized* the generation of these products and services, while, at the same time, it had *allowed* the privately provided new outputs to benefit from some monopoly protection that, at least initially, it provided to intellectual property. This was happening at a time when tax rates on the profits generated, including on those from the newly created "monopolies," were being sharply reduced.

The newly produced goods and services could be sold, worldwide, at conditions determined by the private sellers, without official controls, and in a world that, because of the recent policy changes, had become more open, thus making the accessible market much broader than it had been in the past. Clearly, the economic environment had become more attractive for some clever and lucky individuals, especially for those who had been able to create intellectually based, global monopolies. These included Apple, Facebook, Twitter, Google, Tesla, and several others.

Unlike the monopolies that had existed a century earlier, which had eventually come to be regulated by governments, the new monopolies were at least initially "protected" by governments, were little or not at all regulated, and the profits derived from them were often little, or hardly, taxed, because of recent tax rules that had made it possible for the owners of these enterprises to avoid paying the taxes on their profits or paying the previous tax rates, which had been much higher.

For all the above reasons, it can be argued that the profits from these activities had become, at least in part, *rents*, in a strictly economic defin-ition of that concept, for those who received them. There was thus a moral, if not a legal, case to share those profits with the society at large, either directly or, at least, through higher (or normal) taxes on their profits. Instead, in the 1980s, the statutory taxes had been sharply reduced. In some cases, such as Apple, there would be antitrust complaints, directed at some aspects of their market behavior, but often little concrete action would come from these complaints.

The conversion, partly or totally, of genuine economic gains into rents happened for several reasons and in several areas, including sports activities, the generation of new drugs, and personal services, such as those provided by Microsoft, Apple, Amazon, Facebook, Google, Twitter, etc.

The sales by the companies that sold mainly newly created *services* had often one of the two characteristics of classic "public goods" that had been identified by Paul Samuelson, in his 1954 article. New users could be added at zero or at very low, marginal costs. However, unlike the pure public goods of traditional public finance theory, described by Samuelson, access to them could be prevented by the providers. Therefore "free riding" was not possible for the outputs of these companies, as it would have been for "pure public goods." This made it possible for the companies that provided these goods and services to sell them to very wide, global audiences, which allowed the companies to get earnings that made their owners very rich. Some of today's richest individuals in the world became so rich in this way.

The governments of larger economies (that of the United States, but also Japan, Germany, the United Kingdom, South Korea, and, in more recent years, China and some others) especially had often financed the basic research that, with its theoretical output, had made possible the generation of the fundamental knowledge that, in turn, had led to the creation of the new intellectually based products and services.

For a recent example, the new vaccines, that were developed at a remarkably quick pace against the COVID-19 pandemic, produced by private pharmaceutical companies, and sold at prices that they determined, generating large profits for them, had been made possible by the previous, extensive, fundamental knowledge over many years that had been available free to anyone who could use it. The output of that research (that could not be protected by patents because of its theoretical nature) had become a true, global public good, one available free to anyone capable of using it for some practical purposes.

Some of that basic knowledge had been obtained at institutions such as the National Institute of Health, in the United States, and at other similar leading public institutions, or at major universities, where the researchers had been partly or fully funded by government grants (see Kolata and

Mueller, 2022). The same had happened in the past, in connection with the discovery of the transistor (that would lead to many commercial, electronic applications that have revolutionized many areas), the Internet, and other discoveries.

The *basic* or *fundamental* research in biology had been mainly directed toward the development of *general* biological knowledge, knowledge that might become useful in dealing with known "risks" (illnesses such as cancers, heart disease, and others), more than for developing knowledge that could be useful against "uncertain" dangers, such as those that future pandemics could bring. See Knight (1964) and Tanzi (2022) for the difference between *risky* and *uncertain* events.

Fundamental or basic research cannot make the above distinction in any specific way, but it can play a fundamental role in opening doors for future, specific applications, including the creation of new drugs or therapies that can help against specific diseases and for developing vaccines against future pandemics. There are many such drugs that are being developed at this time, to deal with specific diseases, such as Alzheimer's, and some forms of cancer. They will be sold by the enterprises capable of developing them.

The research on the nature of DNA has been one of these fundamental research outputs over past decades. It opened the way to the generation of vaccines and new cures (such as gene therapy) that could be used against known and previously unknown illnesses, including pandemics. As mentioned, the research that led to the creation of the Internet, had originally had military objectives, as had the research that led to GPS. These new instruments would find private uses and applications, leading to high profits for some private entrepreneurs.

Starting especially in the 1980s onward, there had been several important policy changes aimed at removing major obstacles to some private economic activities that had existed. Some of these changes would be important in facilitating the creation of the new, private "rents" that would become large in later years and include individuals from different countries. In the words of *The Economist* magazine, "adventure capitalism" would become global.

The creation of *"investment hubs,"* in places such as Silicon Valley, in California, Cambridge, in Massachusetts, Oxford, in the United Kingdom, and other places where individuals with a lot of money to invest and inventors from major universities with new ideas trying to find financial backing for the possible commercial use of some of their new discoveries would come into easy and frequent contact, would be one of the important outgrowths of recent developments. These "investment hubs" had not existed, or had been much less important, in the distant past. They would be facilitated by the creation of *elite networks*, which in more recent years have included very rich individuals willing to risk parts of their wealth to finance some risky investments with high, potential, but uncertain, returns. In the distant past more primitive forms of "investment hubs" might have been some coffee houses in London, and some other places, where investors met and considered risking some money in insuring some risky activities such as commercial ships. The private insurance market had come into existence in this way.

We shall provide just a few examples of some of the important policy changes that were made. There were more than the ones reported. Some of them had started to be introduced in the late 1970s. Others were introduced in the 1980s and later years, when market fundamentalism was more directly influencing policy decisions and developments.

In 1982, for the first time, US corporations were allowed to buy their own shares from the stock market. This policy change became progressively more attractive to corporations and to their managers when, in later years, credit that could be used to buy the shares became cheaper because of the policies followed by the central banks and when the compensation of the managers came to be increasingly tied to the short run value of the shares. Cheap credit in the 1990s allowed the managers of many corporations to purchase shares of their own companies with, easily obtainable, borrowed funds. These actions contributed to increase the net-of-tax compensation of the managers, as well as the returns to the shareholders, and contributed to making the income distribution less even.

That policy change helped reduce the tax liabilities, because the interest payments were deductible expenses for tax purposes, while the unrealized capital gains that they generated to the shareholders were not taxed. This treatment of interest payment would also contribute to maintaining pressures by the corporate sector on the Federal Reserve System to keep providing cheap credit in future years.

The large fall in marginal tax rates, that took place after the 1986 "Fundamental Tax Reform" by the Reagan Administration, would add additional pressures on the Federal Reserve to keep interest rates low, as it generally did in the years that followed. Many "structural" changes were also made in the tax systems, such as making depreciation allowances for capital expenses more generous for tax purposes, converting parts of the managers' compensation into low-taxed capital gains, thus changing, for tax purposes, the composition of the total compensations that the managers received for their performances and the reduction in the marginal tax rates.

Some of these changes, which, at times, seemed to be simple, minor reinterpretations of existing laws and did not attract much attention when they were made, came on top of: the sharp reductions in the marginal tax rates on taxable incomes; the large increases in the managers' compensations that were taking place in those years; and the deregulation of many markets, including those that promoted "shadow banking" activities and more global activities.

Legitimate (as distinguished from illegal) "shadow banking" had hardly existed before. Its activity helped create huge compensation for some financial operators in hedge funds, equity funds, and investment banks, institutions that increasingly engaged in risky financial operations (see Briody, 2003). Some of these operations had more similarity with betting in a casino than with genuine investing. Their activities were based on the expectation that the costs at which the borrowing was done would remain low, while the rates at which the money was lent would remain high, and that the creditors would remain solvent. Significant changes in nominal interest rates could, thus, create great wealth repercussions.

In those years the sharp separation that had existed between "commercial banks" and "investment banks" was eliminated, making many banking activities riskier. Being able to take more risks and spreading it was considered an important aspect of a free market, one that, by spreading the risk, would contribute to the efficiency of the economy and to economic growth. Search for efficiency became a major mover.

The above developments and others, some to be discussed in later chapters, and their impact on after-tax personal incomes, led to the large increases in the Gini coefficients that were recorded in the years that followed. These increases created pools of super rich individuals in search of new investment opportunities for their money (the "venture capitalists"). It also contributed to the growing skepticism, among many in the general public, about the claimed "fairness" of the capitalist system, given the way the market economy was operating and was compensating different participants (managers versus workers) for their efforts.

The fairness claims about the results of the free market sounded increasingly hollow to many. This was especially the case when the high gains were seen as being due more to luck, to personal connections, to initial positions, and to acts of corruption, including various kinds of insider trading, than to genuine and sustained effort, by those who received the high compensations.

A market is never and can never be totally free, as some libertarian economists have continued to believe that it can be. It always operates within some visible and some less visible rules, rules that help some individuals and enterprises more than others. With time, these rules tend to favor more those who have held power, the rich, because they have had the funds to buy favors from politicians and from public administrators, those who have influence on the creation and the interpretation of the existing rules. The normal development has been the informal creation of elite networks, networks of individuals with broadly similar interests, that benefit from the rules and the connections. They are the ones who have the power to influence the rules and to make them more favorable to them.

Often former politicians and public administrators find well-paying jobs in the much better paying private enterprises that they had been regulating, and to which they had made favors. These individuals bring with them their knowledge and especially their personal contacts, that are very valuable to their new employers. This happens during normal times, times that can last long periods. The situation only changes during wars, great depressions, or revolutions, when capital may be destroyed, networks may cease to exist, unemployment may go up, and high incomes may disappear.

As it was working during the years since the 1980s, the capitalist system and the market had departed in significant ways from the way theorized by Hayek, Von Mises, Friedman, and others, and as it had been described in Stigler's (1975) popular textbook on "Price Theory." In the way the system had been described by these leading economists, in an efficient market elites and special rules, designed to favor some over others, did not exist. Therefore, they did not play any role. The rules that existed affected everyone in the same way, and incomes and prices were determined by traditional and well-behaved demand and supply curves that determined the market prices for all the goods that individuals bought.

In recent times, well behaved demand and supply curves seem to determine the prices of a small and decreasing share of what individuals spend money on. Much of their spending does not go to products or services that can be bought in granular amounts. Today, many expenses go to goods and services that must be bought in fixed amounts. Expenses for the payment of income and property taxes, rents, tuitions, plane tickets, memberships to clubs, purchase of cars, payments for vacation packages, etc. come in fixed amounts. And some markets are distorted by publicity or in other ways.

The spending power of a person and the costs of what is purchased still influence the expenses of individuals, but not in the granular way assumed by traditional supply and demand theory. This means that loss of spending power by an individual cannot be met by simply reducing the amounts or the quality of what is bought or by "tightening the traditional belt." It often has more drastic and painful consequences.

As mentioned, some of the large "incomes" in recent times were made possible, at least indirectly, by the government-financed basic research, changes in policy rules, and past *public* investments. And some had been promoted by lobbying or similar developments in the political sphere, rather than by the personal efforts of those who received these incomes. See Tanzi (2014b) for an early discussion of this point.

The very high, modern "incomes," or better the "compensations," received by managers and by some others have been inviting negative reactions, especially when they are also subjected to the low marginal tax rates of recent decades or when they totally escape taxation, as they do at times, because of tax evasion or tax avoidance, facilitated by the complexity of modern tax rules, global activities, and tax competition.

To give an idea of how much things have changed, the 1986 US tax reform reduced the US highest marginal tax rate on personal income, the rate that at one time, in the United States and the United Kingdom, had exceeded 90 percent and had inspired the Beatles' song, *The Taxman* in the 1960s, to 28 percent in the United States. After 1986, being very rich had become much more pleasant, more rewarding, and more influential in politics.

In recent years, the skepticism about how the capitalist system and the market were working became more pronounced among the general population. It has been promoting more populist reactions in several countries, including the United States and the United Kingdom. If these reactions are not contained, they risk leading to, and generating, undesirable consequences in future years, as happened at various times and in several countries in the past. The 2023 Davos meeting has reflected these preoccupations.

An important consequence of the developments of recent decades has been that life expectancy in the United States has not increased in the past ten years because the mortality rates between different classes have become very divergent. They have continued to increase among those with high incomes and have fallen among the less well to do, because of differences in smoking habits, use of opioid products, suicide, and homicides (see Marquez, 2023). As an extreme example, the difference in life expectancy between Chevy Chase, a rich area of the Washington metropolitan area, and Anacostia, a poor area just about ten miles away, is now an extraordinary thirty years.

20

Intellectual Property and Venture Capitalists

"Perfect storms" do occasionally occur in our world, both atmospheric and figurative ones. These storms usually include various elements that at times combine in unanticipated ways to contribute to the storms' total power. A perfect storm started forming in the late 1970s/early 1980s in the United States, the United Kingdom, and in some other economies. Some of the elements of that storm are mentioned here, without much elaboration.

Some of those elements were the direct consequence of the "market fundamentalist" movement that had come to influence not only the economic policies but, perhaps as importantly, also the general attitudes of many individuals, starting in the second half of the 1970s. Some of the elements had originated from new technologies that had started earlier on a smaller scale but that acquired more importance in the later years.

An element that would become particularly important was the economic role played by the expanding and government-protected concept of "intellectual property." Intellectual property had, of course, existed in the past, but it had played a less important role, because the creation of new technologies that needed government protection had been less significant and the economic value of intellectual property that had been directly derived from it had been generally small. This could be seen from the limited number of patents that had been requested and given in the past, and that had often been identified with the names of specific individuals, such as Thomas Edison. Few very rich individuals in the past had acquired their wealth directly from intellectual capital.

Intellectual capital status had played a relatively minor role in generating very large fortunes during the years of the Industrial Revolution, compared with the role that had been played by the ownership of, or the access to, *tangible* capital. In the distant past it was tangible capital that had been used to attract the financing needed for making productive investments, as had then been investments in railroads, steel mills, electricity, and new machines, for example.

That financing had come mainly from banks, or occasionally from very rich individuals. During the late twentieth century, and the early part of the twenty-first century, because of the growing role of "venture capitalists," individuals who had large incomes and had acquired great wealth could afford to invest parts of their wealth into risky ventures with great potential returns. Investments in new digital and medical technologies had increased significantly. In later years the role of venture capitalists would become more global (see *The Economist*, November 27–December 3, 2021).

After the Second World War and during the Cold War years that followed a lot of research had been sponsored by government agencies and, in the United States, much had been directed toward military applications or toward the activities by the National Aeronautics and Space Administration (NASA). A good share of this research had been in engineering areas and some had digital applications in the new semiconductor industry that had come into existence near San Francisco.

At that time, Gordon E. Moore had made a prediction that would prove to be accurate. The prediction was that the number of transistors that could be crammed on a chip of silicon would double every two years. This would become Moore's Law. Today billions of transistors can be fitted on a chip. A Nobel winning Physicist, William Shockley, would contribute to this new area and would open the "Shockley Semiconductor" in Mountain View near San Francisco. That would be followed by the "Fairchild Semiconductor," led by Bob Noyce, who had been the inventor of the microchip. Noyce and Moore went on to create Intel (see Miller, 2022).

Research of a biological or natural science type, connected with the aging of the population, and with some related illnesses, also became more important in those years and led to the understanding and decoding of the DNA, that would, later, lead to many applications in the biological and medical field, and create many new investment opportunities.

In those early years an important role had been played by the Engineering Department of the University of Stanford, in California. Researchers at that University had been encouraged to think of commercial applications for their research findings, that would help justify the large amount of money that the US Defense Department and the National Aeronautical and Space Administration (NASA) had been spending in financing research. In those years the potential economic importance of "intellectual property" would become increasingly evident, and that importance would grow dramatically with the passing of years.

Initially, research connected with digital technology which could lead to the creation of many new important enterprises would be a priority. That applied research would give the area around Stanford and the Bay of San Francisco the name of *Silicon Valley*, due to the use of silicon in semiconductors. The Fairchild Semiconductor (FCS) had been one of the first and most successful Venture Capital Start Ups in Silicon Valley and remained very important in this area.

The experience of the Hub in Silicon Valley that included Stanford and Berkeley universities would spread to some other areas, such as Cambridge, Massachusetts, where MIT and Harvard were located, to the area around the University of North Carolina, to Oxford in the United Kingdom, and to other areas. It would involve digital technology and investments in biological and natural sciences and various areas of artificial intelligence. With the passing of the years, the research would expand to "digital assets," including Crypto assets, which would attract many investors. The very first example of a venture capital has been traced as far back as 1946, with the American Research and Development Corporation (ARDC).

Venture capitalists became increasingly attracted by the future, potential profits that new intellectual capital (initially protected by patents) could generate. The number of these capitalists increased in the 1980s onward. Scientists in leading universities realized that some of their scientific findings could not just give them a reputation among their academic colleagues, as they had done in the past, but could have practicable applications that could make them rich. This was a relatively new cultural development, especially on a large scale that became increasingly important in the 1980s and in later years.

In addition to the United States and the United Kingdom, other countries, such as Japan, Germany, South Korea, and increasingly China and India, were also acquiring more patents, more copyrights, and other claims over new forms of intellectual capital. Private institutions came into existence to help potential inventors to acquire the intellectual rights for their discoveries. The National Venture Capital Association was founded in the United States in 1973.

As the number of rich individuals would grow during the years of market fundamentalism, especially in the United States and the United Kingdom in the 1980s and 1990s, more financial resources would become available for these investments. For some rich individuals, an alternative channel to invest some of their large wealth in was the art market. The prices of art objects, especially paintings by well-known artists, would reach record levels. Demand from rich individuals would play a growing role in determining the value of works by new artists, as compared with the distant past, when the general public had played more of a role, with its preferences, in determining the importance of works of art and of artists.

"Digital assets" have also become increasingly important in determining total wealth in recent years. Increasingly they have attracted investors who like gambling, hate government interventions, and hope to make easy gains. Recently (November 2022) "digital assets" ran into major difficulties, and investments in one of their companies suffered major losses.

As mentioned earlier in this chapter, much relatively new basic or fundamental knowledge was available and freely accessible to anyone in the world who was sophisticated enough to understand it and to develop practical ways to use it. Scientific meetings and publications, that reported and made available that knowledge, had become more widely accessible in an increasingly globalized and more educated world, and so was access to advanced schools in several countries by able students from any country. Over those years, the number of foreign students, especially from China, that went to study in top foreign schools was in the millions. They brought back to their countries a lot of technical knowledge. Mobility of able scientists also increased as many gravitated to the major investment hubs. This created a new culture, especially in Silicon Valley.

The freely available theoretical capital had created a potentially fertile hunting ground for new, practical innovations and for new economic possibilities for lucky, clever, well-connected, and well financed individuals. They could exploit it to establish claims for new valuable products and especially new *services* that, at least initially, could benefit from the protection given to patentable "intellectual properties." Later, the enterprises created could also benefit from their size and their expertise, which would make free entry for others more difficult.

By that time, there were many new, very rich and well-connected individuals ready to risk some of their large wealth to exploit the new possibilities. In those years, the world markets had also become much wider for them, because of globalization, that had opened the existing frontiers to the sale of the new products or services and to foreign investments. This had created a kind of multiplier effect. In a more open world the new services and products could be sold globally, rather than just nationally as they had been sold before, making their sale potentially more profitable.

Silicon Valley in California, Cambridge in Massachusetts, Oxford in the United Kingdom, and some other places in China, India, Korea, and elsewhere became major *investments hubs*. In these hubs, financial and technological elites could easily establish contacts and relate to one another, especially during the years of market fundamentalism and globalization. Some of them would succeed in creating what would become enormously successful companies.

New *Elite Networks* facilitated the contacts between the academic inventors, often individuals from major universities who had the new, original ideas, but had limited market sophistication and financial means, and the rich individuals who, given their large wealth, could easily take risks with parts of it, by investing in several new projects. Some consulting enterprises also came into existence to facilitate these contacts. The expectation was that, while some or many of these investments might fail, the few that succeeded would generate very high returns and compensate the investors for the failures.

A relevant question that might be raised is: would these investments have been made if the rich individuals had not existed? And, if not, would this have delayed the scientific and technological progress that took place in several areas, and especially the progress that made possible the creation of new digital enterprises and new drugs? Without that progress, would the world be better or worse off? Or looking at it from a different angle, did the prospects of high profits and the existence of many rich individuals distort the allocation of investments, by giving a preference for discoveries that would help richer users of the results, over results that would have helped poorer individuals, such as dealing with malaria and other diseases that affect mostly poorer people? These are important questions that are not easy to answer.

Some clever people who saw an opportunity at the right time, such as Gates, Jobs, Zuckerberg, Bezos, and Musk, took advantage of these development and created new enterprises, that, over the years, became important and very profitable. Some of these enterprises became the most profitable enterprises in the world, and the individuals who had created them became as fabulously rich as had been the "robber barons" of the Industrial Revolution.

These individuals met informally and socially, in private clubs, or in more formal meetings, as were the annual meetings in Davos, the Milken conferences in California, or scientific–financial meetings in other places. For example, the May 2–3, 2022 meeting, organized by the Milken Institute, in Los Angeles, was appropriately named "Celebrating the Power of Connection." Connections had obviously acquired significant economic power.

Several of the most profitable enterprises in the world in recent years have had an origin different from those that had existed a century or more ago. Most of them produce *intangible* services or new products that much depend on the *information* that they contain, rather than on their *material inputs.* Some produce material products that also depend a lot on the new intellectual capital that they contain, rather than on their raw labor and the tangible inputs (such as steel, copper, land, etc.). Some of these new services had not even been seen as needed by most people, before they were created, unlike the products that had been produced by the capitalists of the Industrial Revolution, which generally had been clearly needed before they were produced and had previously been very expensive to buy.

However, the money value generated by the sale of the new services and products, and the prevailing accounting convention that economists and statisticians had developed in the past, gave the same weight and value to each dollar created by the new services and products, such as those of Facebook, Twitter, or Apple, as to products such as bread or steel, or the transportation services of railroads and other means. These measurement standards might puzzle some common individuals and probably might have puzzled Adam Smith.

The new outputs include micro, or smart, phones, laptops, Apple watches, computers, electric cars, and others. Or, simply, they produce services that convey information to their users through digital applications, including people's views on various issues. The value of the new, big enterprises of today is mostly based on their ownership of some intellectual capital and on the income that they generate with their large sales. It is not based on the ownership of land, buildings, mines, or raw materials, as it had been years ago, and especially during the Industrial Revolution. It is now based on the ability to provide services that carry information and that facilitate *connectivity*, which may at times be very valuable or at times worthless or even damaging in connectivity with strangers.

Connectivity has increased in recent years, connectivity with family and friends but also connectivity with perfect strangers. Those who use Twitter or Facebook often do not know one another. The new tools have made it easier for anyone to contact, and at times influence, perfect strangers including children. There are obvious benefits and costs associated with these contacts.

The leading companies of today require far less *real* investment (and savings to finance investment) and often far less workers than did the old-style companies of the past. Some have billion dollar profits with a few thousand employees and little capital.

Some of the new applications that use Artificial Intelligence are aimed at saving labor, leading to the question of the jobs that will be available to workers in the future, when robots are likely to take many of the places of today's workers. Although the future is difficult to pierce, it is easy to be pessimistic and to wonder what jobs will be available to the workers who lose their job but need to provide an income? Experiences of the past may not be relevant in the future.

In a lecture that Larry Summers gave at the International Monetary Fund, on November 3, 2016, he provided some interesting data on the comparison between the market capitalization and the value of property, plants, and equipment for old style companies (such as Exon, GM, and Walmart) and for new intellectual capital-based companies (Amazon, Apple, Facebook, Google, and others). The original data came from Bloomberg. The multiples between market capitalization and needed property, plant, and equipment, for old style companies and new companies were extraordinarily different. For the first group, they ranged from 1.4 to 2.5. For the second group the market capitalization ranged from 18 to 65 of the value of the real properties. Most of the profits for the second group came from the value of the intellectual capital that they incorporated and not from that of the real, tangible capital that they owned. But profits were profits and the profits of both went into the determination of the countries' GDPs and the owners' wealth.

The new enterprises had initially been started by individuals with new, potentially useful ideas and with little initial money, such as Jobs, Gates, Zuckerberg, and others. They had been able to get access to the financial capital needed to develop their ideas and had made the ideas economically profitable. Often, the needed capital had been provided by "venture capitalists" rather than from traditional commercial banks, as had generally been the case in the past, when the loans had been obtained from banks, such as the Morgan Bank, making the banks very powerful.

Some well-placed, smart, perseverant, but also lucky, individuals were able to extract huge gains from what were, at the beginning, de facto, unregulated, but government protected, modern monopolies. Luck and perseverance, and access to financial capital, seem to have played important roles in many of these successes. This was the case with Microsoft, Apple, Google, Facebook, Twitter, and other similar companies.

The new rich individuals have not only accumulated huge wealth and formed elite networks that make it easier for them to interact with other rich people with similar goals, and to influence the individuals who make the rules, or can interpret the existing rules (as politicians and high-level public administrators often do) – they have also tried to control some of the means of communication, so that they can more easily influence general public opinions and, through them, policies and markets. Many of the large means of communication are today owned by some of the richest men.

The richest men, and they are often men, first bought some of the major newspapers, magazines, and radio stations, and then expanded in other areas, including cable television channels and other more modern means, such as Twitter. They had learned an important lesson from Napoleon, who had stated that "four hostile newspapers are more to be feared than 1000 bayonets."

As a recent newspaper article put it, "Technological change and the fortunes it created have given a … small club of massively wealthy individuals the ability to play arbiters, moderators and bankroller of not only the information that feeds the nation's discourse but also the architecture that undergirds it" (Scherer and Ellison, 2022, p. 1). The richest individuals in the United States have "… autonomy over the algorithms and moderation policies of the nation's top three social media platforms, Facebook, Instagram and Facebook Messenger." "The information that courses over these networks is increasingly produced by publications controlled by fellow billionaires …" (Ibid.).

The conclusion of that interesting article was that "… we are now very dependent on the personal whims of rich people, and there are few checks and balances on them. They could lead [us] in a liberal, conservative or libertarian direction, and there is very little we can do about that" (Ibid., p. 4). Just think of Musk's current global reach and his implicit "political" power.

So much for the dream of a completely free and libertarian market economy, one without controls that would promote freedom and social welfare *for all*. The question of whether there is now some need to control the *market* in some way as, over the centuries, many had thought that there had been the need to control the power of the *government* (see Gordon, 1999) has become an increasingly relevant and urgent one. There also remains a high controversy as to whether this control is needed and, if it is, how should it be achieved.

Another important issue is that, because of the changed policies and technological environment over the past half century, in many cases the same genuine effort by an individual, say a top athlete, an effort that in the past would have earned that individual a modest, but a fully deserved income, have led to earnings that can be in the millions of US dollars. This leads to the inevitable questioning of the full economic legitimacy of those earnings for those who receive them. For a real-life example, related to a top tennis player, of earnings that could be considered partly rents, see Tanzi (2018a, ch. 30).

In a strictly economic sense, some of the new, inflated earnings could be considered, at least partly, "rents," rather than genuine "incomes." In the past some economists had objected to the existence of rents, as for example rents derived from inheritances, considering them not genuinely "deserved." In today's world, the "rent" part of the total compensation of some individuals has been provided by society at large, and not by the effort of the individuals, or even by that of their ancestors, as was the case with rents from inherited property. The same effort and the same ability by an individual a century ago, would have generated that individual a far lower compensation, but one that would have been considered, and would have been, an undisputable income, and not rent.

This is a fundamental aspect of economics that has deep implications for equity and that would seem to merit more attention by economists than it has received so far. Does a capitalist system where such rents have become important have the same legitimacy as one where all compensations reflect genuine efforts? Most normal or dependent workers have not benefited from these developments. On the contrary, as workers, rather than as consumers, some have been hurt by globalization, and by the loss of jobs to automation. The "rent" part of their compensation may even have become negative. This was not the way the capitalist system had been assumed to work.

The change, over the years, in compensation for the same performance for some categories of individuals (say free agents versus workers) could be attributed to public policies, that, through public spending, had, first, financed the generation of some fundamental, basic knowledge and then had protected the intellectual property rights of the "secondary" or "derived" knowledge made possible by the original and publicly financed fundamental one. Cultural changes had also played an important role, as we have shown.

Governments had financed much (though not all) of the basic research that had been instrumental in making the creation of the new platforms (radio, television, internet, GPS, etc.) that had allowed the performance, in our example, of the tennis player to be sold to millions of individuals worldwide, rather than to just a few hundred local spectators. The same power was given to many enterprises (Facebook, Twitter, and others) for selling various services to a worldwide audience, in a global market.

Because of technological developments, such as the transistor, the Internet, and, for basic biological research, DNA and other advances, it has become possible for some individuals and for some enterprises to generate products and especially services that can be patented and sold to billions of buyers, in a world that, also because of changes in policies, has become more globalized, so that far more customers than in the past can be reached. Furthermore, some of the sales are now made not directly to the consumers of those products but to advertisers, who use the platforms to advertise various consumer products. The final users may feel that they are getting these services free, which is a further distortion of the market.

Today, drugs that require doctors' prescriptions to use, and even some hospital surgical procedures, are advertised directly to the patients, rather than to the doctors. Clearly, this is no longer Adam Smith's, or Hayek's, or Stigler's market, and we should recognize the changes that have taken place and their economic importance. Now, demand and supply schedules may tell us much less that they did a century ago about consumer demands.

Some lucky individuals and enterprises can now extract huge profits from large sales, profits that, because of complex tax laws, and because of low tax rates on high incomes, are taxed much less than they were fifty years ago. Some of the largest enterprises in the world today seem to have the intellectual–capital characteristics that were described. They sell services with techniques that were derived from government-provided basic intellectual capital, using protected intellectual property, and the profits are taxed at low rates. One of these enterprises, Apple, in early 2020, became the largest enterprise in the whole world, in term of capitalization, taking the place that many years ago had been occupied by US Steel.

We are now at a time when the action of individuals has generated climate changes but also generated major and not always easy to comprehend changes in the market economy. Let us not make the double mistake of assuming that neither the natural world nor the economic world need policy changes.

2 1

The World in the Twenty-First Century

By the beginning of the twenty-first century the world had really changed in many ways, especially in favor of rich individuals. A question to raise is whether the enterprises and the high-income individuals who had mostly benefited from the changes should not share some of their (partly or mostly *rental*) gains with the rest of society (both the national and even the global society) in which they live. We shall be repeating to some extent some of the conclusions of the two earlier chapters.

The domestic sharing could be done simply through higher taxes on higher incomes or in other more difficult ways. This would allow governments to more easily help the workers who have been the losers in these developments and to provide better universal protection against risks that all individuals (rich and poor, regardless of their racial or ethnic background) face. These risks include illnesses, old age, and insufficient education. Recent US surveys have indicated that Americans now expect enterprises to do more than they have in past years to deal with social ills. This contrasts with the view, pushed by Milton Friedman in the 1970s, that had become popular in the 1980s and 1990s, that the only responsibility that enterprises have is toward their shareholders.

There is no question that new knowledge is needed in today's world to address the difficult issues raised by recent developments, just as Keynes had thought in 1926. A continuation of current trends is not likely to lead to a good destination, and the solutions are not likely to be simple ones, such as increasing public spending or allowing more libertarian policies to prevail. They will need hard thinking and new knowledge.

Another important change has been the novel view, promoted by some economists, especially in the 1970s and 1980s, that financial incentives have a great impact on the performance and the productivity of individuals who manage enterprises and money or on the productivity of other individuals who can act independently. Money compensation, and not duty, personal pride, reputation, or intellectual curiosity, was suggested to be the main or sole driving force in the performances of these individuals; and that the higher was the promised or expected money compensation, the better was the expected personal performance.

Another closely related aspect of the above view was that high taxes on these individuals have a negative effect on their incentives and reduce their performances and the productivity of the economy. Therefore, high tax rates are always bad, regardless of how the revenues are collected or used, while high net-of-tax compensations, for individuals in particular positions, are always good. The higher is the net-of-tax compensation, the better will be the performance of the individual and the economy.

Strangely this view was not assumed to apply to dependent workers, but only to managers and other independent performers. Therefore, the earnings of dependent workers could be constrained, or squeezed, as much as possible, to allow the higher compensations for the few lucky ones (mostly managers, share owners, and some free agents). And earnings of workers *were* squeezed. For many workers, real wages remained unchanged for decades.

The above view of personal behavior and performance in capitalist systems, a view that had not prevailed in the previous decades, 1940s until the 1960s, had originated in the second half of the 1970s, and had become popular in in the 1980s. That view seemed to have first appeared in 1974, in Washington, in the form of a curve, drawn on a restaurant napkin by Arthur Laffer, a conservative economist, during a lunch with a group of leading conservative politicians. It came to be called the "Laffer Curve" and it would have much influence, especially on US policy makers, in the years that followed.

The Laffer Curve became a gospel for conservative economists, for some government officials, and for most rich individuals. It was also dismissed, or ridiculed, by less conservative ones. The reported reaction of Paul Samuelson, when he was first told about the Laffer Curve, may be worth reporting. It had been that: "the Laffer curve is good for a good laugh." David Stockman, Budget Director during the Reagan Administration, would describe Laffer as "a charlatan who claims to be an economist" (see Schwartzman, 2022).

In spite of these unfavorable comments, the curve became a very influential concepts in economics and Laffer received the Presidential

Medal of Freedom from President Trump. It has also been reported that he has been earning up to a million dollars a year in speaking fees. Clearly many have continued to believe in the wisdom of using low marginal tax rates on high income individuals and low taxes on corporations to extract good performances from them.

In the early years when tax rates were still high, the Laffer Curve was an indirect element that helped justify the asking for and the giving of what would become increasingly high, or even absurdly high compensations, including large bonuses and free corporate shares, that became common and that were given to CEOs and other managers and other individuals in particular positions in the industrial, financial, entertainment, and professional sectors. Even managers of non-profit organizations and of sport teams, and some university presidents, ended up getting million dollar compensations in the new environment. High taxes called for higher gross compensations to compensate some categories of citizens. That libertarian view has continued to push for the further slashing of higher tax rates for high incomes until the current times.

The libertarian view promoted and encouraged the squeezing of the wages of normal, dependent workers, a process that was facilitated by the ongoing globalization trend and by the accompanying weakening of the labor unions taking place since the 1970s, especially in the Unites States and the United Kingdom. For average workers, financial incentives, or higher wages, were not assumed to have any stimulating effect on their productivity. Those effects were assumed to exist only for managers, and for some other lucky individuals.

It is not likely that Adam Smith would have endorsed these developments, that were attributed to the way capitalism was supposed to work. Like robots, normal workers were not supposed to respond to higher compensation, and statutory minimum wages remained low. Their existence continued to be opposed by the managers of enterprises and to be criticized by conservative economists, because they interfered with the work of the free market.

For the managers and other individuals in similar positions, there was no optimal, upper limit to the sizes of the bonuses and the compensations that were supposed to stimulate better performances. The larger were the compensations, the better was the expected productivity of the managers, without limits. With time some of those compensations would become so large as to appear absurd.

The average compensation of corporate managers rose from five times the average wages of workers, the level that the first Nobel Prize Winner in Economics, Ian Tinbergen, had considered desirable in the 1950s, and from the about twenty times the level that had been assumed desirable by Peter Drucker, the famed, US management expert in the 1960s, to levels that, at times, have reached or exceeded 1,000 times the dependent workers' average wages. For example, today, the CEOs of Starbucks and Chipotle have been reported to earn, respectively, 1,500 and 2,000 times the average salaries of their workers. The CEO of Apple has been reported to receive about 1,500 times the compensation of Apple's dependents. Managers are reported to earn about 600 times the average wages of the workers that they supervise in the United States.

Compensations in many millions or, at times, even in billions of dollars in the financial market have also become less rare and at times even expected and, again, these compensations are now taxed at far lower rates than they had been in the past, in part because of the ways that the compensation packages are now structured, to take advantage of some tax preferences that were introduced in recent decades for some component of compensations, such as "carried trade," delayed compensations that could qualify as capital gain, and others, and in part because of the reduction in the statutory marginal tax rates.

Due to the changed cultural environment, there was no longer any embarrassment on the part of managers to ask for and to expect huge compensations from their often-docile Corporate Boards. On their side, the Boards did not want to be embarrassed by paying *their* managers less than similar corporations were paying *theirs*.

Some managers got these high compensations even when the performances of the enterprises that they managed had been far from admirable. This, for example, happened in Boeing, after two of its new, most advanced planes crashed within a few months, creating a major reputational crisis for that enterprise, in an industry that much depended on technical reputations. Not long after the crashes, the CEO of Boeing retired, but he still retired with tens of millions of dollars, presumably as compensation for his "high productivity" and "good performance"!

In the case of Boeing the close connection between the managers of the enterprise and the regulators seemed to have played a role in allowing planes with potential defects to fly. The connection had largely eliminated the role that regulators are expected to play. It was an example of Elite Networks in action, in an area where it should not have been. The regulatory function of the government had been reduced or eliminated in favor of self-regulation of some enterprises, or of no regulation at all, as libertarians have continued to favor. They have continued to insist that a good capitalist system would prefer no regulations and almost no taxes, because both add costs and reduce individual freedom.

By the way, the experience in Boeing with the regulatory oversight was far from rare. That experience had become increasingly common in our recent, market-fundamentalist world, one that was expected to need little regulation for free men in a capitalist system. Of course, it was expected that the enterprises would know how to regulate themselves, as they had presumably done in the environmental area, in the pharmaceutical area, and as they had done in the smoking era.

The recent experience with opioid medicines has been a recent reminder of how the self-regulation system works or might work. The even more recent experience (December 2022) with Crypto finance and with the regulation, or nonregulation, of FTX has been another. The FTX founder, Sam Bankman-Fried, was reported "to have kept a close relation with the regulators who oversaw the company" (*The Washington Post*, December 14, p. 1).

In the financial market, some individuals have at times gotten million dollars bonuses, also for their good performances, just days before the institutions in which they had been working have declared bankruptcy (see Stenfors, 2017, for examples). If the market is assumed to always be right, as it was supposed to be during the years of "market fundamentalism," and if its outcomes should not be questioned, these compensations were also not to be challenged. They should be assumed to have been fully deserved by those who received them.

Another development had been the already reported major changes in the tax systems, that had occurred in many countries, and especially in the United States and the United Kingdom, in the 1980s onward. Further reductions had been introduced in the United States in 2017, by the Trump Administration, especially for taxes on corporate profits, and conservative economists and managers have continued to believe that these taxes are still too high and discourage investment. Since the Second World War the share of taxes on profits into GDP has fallen from about 5–6 percent to 1–2 percent. The two highest tax rates on corporate income in the United States were reduced from 40/46 in 1986 to 25/34 in 1991 (see Messere, 1993, p 341).

In those years the high, marginal tax rates, the ones that are important for very high income individuals, were dramatically reduced (in the United States from 94 percent in the 1950s to 28 percent in 1987). Taxes on corporations and capital income were also slashed. These reductions were made in the belief that they would stimulate incentives and make the economies more efficient. Many have continued to believe in the merit of this policy.

A detailed analysis of optimal taxation of top labor incomes in several countries, made by leading experts, has shown that the tax rates on the top incomes could be significantly higher, without any negative impact on incentives and performances (see Khaled and De Mooji, 2000; Diamond and Saez, 2011; Piketty, Saez, and Stantcheva, 2014). However, conservatives refuse to accept these results and continue to believe in the magic of the Laffer Curve and to campaign for more tax reductions.

In mid-2022 a newly elected British Prime Minister promised to cut British income taxes in the middle of a fiscal crisis, believing in the magic of tax reduction. She was forced to resign in record time. Clearly the libertarian religion continues to have some convinced disciples.

Growing complexity in the tax systems, a complexity that has increased significantly over the years – because of the many micro changes in the laws or in the interpretations of the existing laws, combined with the effects of globalization on tax systems, and of the new, intellectual services that are now traded – created novel opportunities, for high net-worth individuals and for corporations, to evade taxes by shifting profits to low tax jurisdictions, such as Ireland, or to tax havens.

Within the United States some individuals can avoid state income taxes by shifting residence from taxed to untaxed states. A large part of the empirical power of the Laffer Curve may now come from the existence of tax competition between different jurisdictions.

Given the existing tax competition between countries, and in some countries, such as the United States and Brazil, between the states, tax-payers can now often easily evade, or avoid, some of the high tax rates that they should pay by simply changing residence or shifting profits from high to low tax jurisdictions. Some of the most profitable corporations in the world today have been reported to pay little taxes. Several studies have estimated that the average tax rate on the incomes of billionaires in the United States is now no higher than that of average workers. Buffet had compared his tax burden with the comparable one of his secretary!

Other factors, such as deregulation, especially in the financial market; the weakening of labor unions; some technological developments that are making it easier for enterprises to replace workers with robots; globalization; and others, have also played significant roles in changing the social and the economic landscape that existed a half century ago. Clearly, the harmony that, to some extent, seemed to have existed or, at least to have been approached, in the mid-1960s, between the desired role of the state and that of the market, had been compromised. First by developments in the late 1960s and 1970s, which had reduced the role of the market, and, more fundamentally, later, by some of the policies and views that market fundamentalism had brought in the 1980s onward that had restricted the role of the government.

Around 1995 there had been, again, the impression that views and developments had converged around a different and more libertarian paradigm that seemed to have brought some temporary harmony once again between market and government. Trust in the market had gone up around that time and so had the pressures for a limited government role. But the harmony then reached would last a short time. New problems would soon appear to challenge it.

Can Societies with very uneven income distribution remain democratic? A question to be asked is whether a market economy, in countries that are still basically democratic and where most adult individuals can vote, can continue to retain its legitimacy and the real economic freedom of *all* its participants when the income distribution becomes as uneven as it became in the United States in recent decades, and when it creates a class of privileged individuals (the Davos Guys? The Yachts and Private Planes Guys? The Venture Capitalists? The owners of the Media? Elon Musk?) who, like the nobles of two centuries ago, or the superrich of the "Gilded Age" at the end of the nineteenth century, have acquired enormous economic power, feel that they are different from the rest of the citizens and that they are entitled to their wealth, and feel that their wealth benefits everyone. They have created a world for the rich, a world that is an unreachable dream for most citizens.

Because of that wealth, and because policies have become progressively more complex for the average voters to know and to understand, the rich elites can now more easily influence those who vote or some of those who make the public policies, by financing their political campaigns and activities, and they can influence the general public by buying major means of communications, such as newspapers, television stations, and enterprises such as Twitter, as Musk recently did. Is this the capitalist system that would make all of us free, create opportunities for all, and raise all the boats?

This was in part the situation that had existed in the 1920s in the United States and in some other parts of the world before the Great Depression in the 1930s. This had led to the major changes in the decades that followed that Depression and the Second World War until the 1970s. In 1926, Keynes, a keen market observer, had felt that the system that existed at that time could not continue in the future without major changes to it. He had called for "new knowledge" to deal with the unsustainable situation. Obviously, in his view, the laissez faire system that then existed had not been capable of delivering what was needed. New knowledge is clearly needed again today to suggest what should be done.

This knowledge and new policies should aim at bringing again some harmony between the economic role of the state, a role that many would consider desirable in a society that is still democratic, and the economic results that the capitalist system, as it is now working, delivers, which are far from satisfactory, especially on equity grounds.

In the view of many people, the needed harmony does not exist in many countries, especially in countries such as the United States and the United Kingdom. The growing divisions between classes that exist in these countries are indications of the absence of that harmony. Those divisions generate large differences in life expectancy and in educational and health achievements, and in many other areas. They generate great differences in social classes, and not just differences based on income. Without that harmony, the world risks moving in unpredictable and undesirable directions, as it did in 1917 in Russia and as it did again, in different ways, in the 1930s, in the United States and other countries.

In recent years, several political scientists have been expressing doubts that the United States and even the world have been moving in the right direction. The future has looked increasingly fragile for various reasons (see Tanzi, 2022), challenging the view that progress is inevitable and beneficial for all, as the conservative CATO institution has continued to argue.

The new harmony would need governments less exposed to lobbies; that use less-complex policies, including in taxation, spending, and monetary policies; that have the capacity to regulate efficiently and equitably the work of the market, when it needs regulation; and that use policies that, while they retain the essential role of the market in the allocation of resources and in the basic freedoms that it provides to individuals in their legitimate economic activities, makes the sharing of the national pie more equitable than it has been.

The policies adopted should aim at reducing income inequality to a tolerable, or acceptable, level, but not to a level that would significantly destroy needed economic incentives and reduce responsible personal freedom. What is needed is a *compassionate* capitalistic system, not an indifferent one, and certainly not a centrally planned Marxist system.

However, calling *any* government intervention "socialism," as some libertarians and conservative observers have continued to do, and opposing any tax increases and pushing for and praising all tax reductions, as they have also continued to do, will not help in reaching feasible sustainable solutions. This only contributes to the problem.

At the same time, simply throwing more money on government spending at the problems, as some observers want to do, and as some government did during the COVID-19 years, without changing some of the basic institutions and without making the policies both *more general and less complex* is not likely to be a desirable alternative.

We should aim for a *compassionate* capitalist system, but one with an *efficient* government capable of resisting pressures from lobbies and a relatively free but efficiently controlled market.

In recent decades Scandinavian countries have shown that a "third" or "alternative" way may be possible, because money, while important, is not the only compass that guides, or should guide, all the actions of humans in societies. They have done this by redistributing incomes in efficient ways without controlling the market. Some "efficient inequality" in incomes and in wealth, to compensate for significant, genuine differences in talent, efforts, and risks taken, is useful and must be retained. But too much is not helpful, either to the economy or to society. Some conservative economists have insisted that "Middle-of-the-Road Policies Lead to Socialism." They reach this conclusion because they assume that those policies are limited to price controls and to arbitrary market controls (see, for example, *Two Essays by Ludwig von Mises*, 1988).

In Scandinavian countries, opposition to immigration has recently created some opposition to welfare policies, because the latter help immigrants who have not contributed to the financing of the needed public resources with the present or past taxes that sustain those policies. These immigrants are seen as free riders. This has been leading to some questioning of the still broadly popular social policies. Countries such as Denmark have become models of good economic and social policies and they have remained good models.

The basic goal should be the promotion of what could still be efficient markets; free markets with some inevitable and necessary inequality in incomes and wealth; and markets that would allow reasonable economic growth within a setting considered relatively fair. That is obviously a tall order. The Scandinavian countries have continued to perform at the top places among countries in most of the relevant comparative economic indices, even though they have had some of the highest taxes and public spending levels. For example, Denmark, Sweden, and Finland were in the first eight placed among 165 countries in the Human Freedom Index of 2022, estimated by the conservative Cato and the Frazer Institutes, while the United Kingdom and the United States were in the twentieth and twenty-sixth places.

Perhaps other countries could learn from the Scandinavian countries, unless the conclusion is that Scandinavian citizens are just from another planet. However, as mentioned, the immigration problem is creating some new difficulties on those performances as it has been creating in other countries. There have also been reports of billionaires moving from Norway to Switzerland, motivated by tax reasons.

How much inequality would be required to keep a country's economy efficient might differ among countries, depending on their community spirit and their sense of being nations, rather than just aggregations of unrelated individuals. Neither income equality, as centrally planned economies had intended to achieve but never achieved, nor excessive income inequality, as the United States has now achieved, would be desirable in the long-term. Community spirit deserves to be given more credit and more importance in policies, but not to the point of overwhelming efficiency. Economists do not help by continually praising individualism and unrestrained economic freedom, because individuals do not live in a Robinson Crusoe world. They now live in close urban communities where negative externalities of various kinds are common.

In many countries, tax policies and, perhaps, also spending programs, in recent decades, have not been in line with what was needed. The arguments about the economic inefficiency of high tax rates and tax levels, while they have some merit, were carried too far, while the arguments about "trickle down," from higher expected growth from market fundamentalist policies, were too quickly believed and promoted by economists who should have known better.

Monetary policy has also created difficulties in recent decades. Cheap money was promoted by the argument that it would stimulate employment and growth, while it would not have much effect on inflation and income distribution. Cheap money is likely to have done little to promote growth while, likely, it became an important contributor to inequality and instability, because access to cheap money has not been the same for rich and poor individuals. The poor have not been able to get access to the zero rate loans of recent years. This aspect has received little attention by relevant monetary authorities. Monetary policy is likely to have contributed to future macroeconomic instability and problems, because over the years it promoted more public debt in place of taxes, and debt always affects the future of economies to some extent.

In 2022, inflation reappeared in a menacing manner following the huge increase in public spending in 2020–2021 and the expansion in the money supply in the previous years, creating major challenges for the Federal Reserve Bank, for the European Central Bank, and for other central banks on how to react. There was also much uncertainty for market operators. The Federal Reserve was forced to begin to sharply increase nominal rates but the rates remained below the current rate of inflation. Fears of recession were again mentioned with increasing frequency.

Interesting discussions of past monetary policy in the United States in recent years and of mistakes made, can be read in Leonard (2022) and de Larosière (2022).

A development that became increasingly important in the past half century was the role played by the expanding concept of "intellectual property," a development that was mentioned in previous chapters but that may deserve a bit more attention at the risk of some repetition. That development was not only important in creating high incomes for some individuals but also in determining the composition of output and national incomes of some countries.

Protection of intellectual property, of course, had existed in the past, but its role in directly determining national income had been more limited, as is evident from the number of patents and copyrights that were requested and given in the past often being identified with specific individuals, such as Thomas Edison. Intellectual capital had played a smaller role in generating very large past incomes, compared with the role played by the ownership of tangible capital. It was *tangible* capital that was used to attract the financing needed for making large productive investments a century or more ago, such as investments in railroads, steel mills, bridges, steamships, and others.

During the second half of the twentieth and the first two decades of the twenty-first centuries there was much more investment in generating new *kinds of technological outputs*, especially those connected with *digital technology*, as compared with *concrete* or *tangible* investments.

"Venture capitalists," who had become more important, were increasingly attracted by potential, future profits that intellectual capital could generate. And scientists in leading universities, such as Stanford, Berkley, MIT, Harvard, and Oxford, had realized that some of their scientific findings could find economic applications and generate economic gains. This was happening at a time when high incomes were becoming more attractive because they were taxed much less than in previous years. In addition to the United States, other countries, including especially Japan and China, were acquiring claims over some new intellectual capital in those years.

By that time there were more rich individuals ready to risk some of their large wealth to exploit the new possibilities. Furthermore, because of globalization and the lower tax rates, new outputs could be sold globally, making the sales more valuable.

Silicon Valley, in California, Cambridge, in Massachusetts, Oxford, in the United Kingdom, and other "investments hubs," mostly near major research universities, had come into existence. In these hubs, financial and technological elites could more easily come into contact and establish mutually attractive relations. The networks facilitated the contacts between the academic inventors, who were the individuals from the major universities with the new ideas, and the rich individuals, who had the money to finance them. In the past the scientists had been more isolated in their ivory towers. The expectation was that, while some of the investments would fail, some would generate high financial returns, at a time when wealth had become more important and more desirable, both socially and economically.

Defenders of market fundamentalism would argue that these investments would not have been made if these new, rich and smart individuals had not existed. Would the absence of these individuals have delayed the scientific and technological progress that took place? And, without that progress, would the world be a worse world, and the market a less efficient one? These are interesting questions to which there are no definitive answers.

People such as Gates, Jobs, Zuckerberg, Bezos, and Musk took advantage of these development and created new enterprises that, over the years, became important and profitable and, increasingly, contributed to the growth of the US and other countries' economies. Some of these enterprises, such as Microsoft and Apple, became among the most profitable enterprises in the world, and the individuals who created them became as fabulously rich as the "robber barons" of the Industrial Revolution around 1900. In more recent years some enterprises in China, India, and elsewhere have been equally successful.

These individuals (venture capitalists) meet informally and socially, in private clubs or in more formal meetings, as in the annual meetings in Davos, the Milken conferences in California, or meetings in other places, including those in universities. For example, the 2022 meeting organized by the Milken Institute in Los Angeles, which was already mentioned, was named "Celebrating the Power of Connection." Some "connections" had acquired definite economic power. Connections also helped many enterprises to choose the individuals that they hired to lead them. Most managers were not chosen from among unknown job applicants.

Several of the most profitable enterprises in the world in recent decades have had an origin different from those that had existed a century or more ago. Most of the new enterprises produce *intangible* services rather than *tangible* goods, or products that much depend for their value on the information that they contain, or transfer to users, rather than on the raw, material inputs that they contain.

The value of some of the new products also depends a lot on the new intellectual capital that has gone in their creation, rather than on their raw labor and tangible inputs, such as steel, copper, etc., as it had in the past. These new products include "smart phones," laptops, computers, Apple watches, electric cars, and others. Or simply they are services that convey information using the Internet, as do Facebook and Twitter. Some require "rare metals" which are in scarce supply in few countries and that are becoming progressively more important in today's world.

The value of some of the big enterprises of today is mostly based on their ownership of intellectual capital, and not on their ownership of land, buildings, mines, or raw materials, as they had been during the Industrial Revolution. It often depends on their ability to provide information that some individuals may want, as do Google and smart phones. Some of the leading companies of today require far less *real* or *tangible* investment than did the old-style companies of the past. What they require is mainly new technological ideas and inputs and smart management.

It is not clear what the implication of this change is for the national saving that countries' economies now need. The multiples between the market capitalization of an enterprise and the needed property in plant and equipment for old style companies and for new companies, as were reported in the Larry Summers' lecture at the IMF, have become extraordinarily different. Most of the profits for new enterprises come from the value of their intellectual capital, and not from that of their real capital input. This means that today's economies might need less saving to make needed investments and to sustain a given income level or a given rate of growth.

The importance of the above conclusion has hardly been appreciated or discussed. For example, in the 1950s, US policymakers had become very worried when the steel production of the Soviet Union exceeded that of the United States. Today, such news would leave individuals and governments largely indifferent, being considered unimportant.

These new, modern, and technologically based enterprises had been started initially by individuals with new ideas, such as Gates, Jobs, and Zuckerberg. These individuals had been able to get access to the financial capital needed to make their new ideas economically valuable. The needed financial capital had often been provided by "venture capitalists," rather than by traditional commercial banks, as had been the case in the distant past, when this had made banks, such as the Morgan Bank, so powerful. Venture capitalists are better able to take risks than banks.

Some well-placed, smart, but often also lucky, individuals were able to extract huge gains from what, at the beginning, were de facto unregulated, but government protected, modern monopolies. Luck, perseverance, and connections seem to have played important roles in these successes. We know more about the successes than about the failures in these attempts, as there must have been many.

The successful ones were Microsoft, Apple, Facebook, Twitter, Tesla, and other similar companies. Those successes gave a long and sustained ride to technologically based stocks. However, recently that long ride seemed to have come to a stop when many of those stocks started to run into difficulties. Perhaps the easier opportunities provided by the new technological advances had been largely exploited. It remains to be seen if this is a temporary or a more durable stop.

22

The Impact of New Economic Developments on the Market and Democracy

In early 2022, the richest man on Earth, Elon Musk, had been willing to invest $44 billion to buy Twitter, one of the companies that sell the power to express views and to advertise products to millions of listeners around the world. A century ago, nobody would have thought that an enterprise could sell peoples' views, or that those views could have economic value. Now there are several enterprises that sell information, some useful, some highly questionable, including opinions and "fake news."

Musk's offer was an indication of both his great wealth and the power that rich individuals have now acquired to influence the views of the general public. In some ways, this development must have raised questions about the practical value of the theoretical conception of free market, the one that still assumes that free and atomized competition exists, or can still exist, in today's market and can generate a fair income distribution.

The new rich individuals have not only accumulated huge fortunes and formed elite networks that make it easier for them to interact with other rich people with similar goals and to influence those who make or interpret the existing rules (politicians and high-level public administrators), but they have also, increasingly, tried to control some of the public means of communication so that they can influence public opinions and, through them, the policies that are adopted.

They did this, first, by buying some of the major newspapers, magazines, and radio stations, and then by expanding in other more modern areas, including cable television channels, and more recent means of communication, such as Twitter and Facebook.

As an article in the *Washington Post* of May 1, 2022 put it, "Technological change and the fortunes it created have given a ... small club of massively wealthy individuals the ability to play arbiters, moderators and bankroller of not only the information that feeds the nation's discourse but also the architecture that undergirds it" (Scherer and Ellison, 2022, p. 1).

The richest individuals have "... autonomy over the algorithms and moderation policies of the nation's top three social media platforms, Facebook, Instagram and Facebook Messenger." "The information that courses over these networks is increasingly produced by publications controlled by fellow billionaires..."

The conclusion of that article was that "... we are now very dependent on the personal whims of rich people, and there are few checks and balances on them. They could lead [us] in a liberal, conservative or libertarian direction, and there is very little we can do about that." (Ibid., p. 4). In other words, we are a long way from the ideal, perfect market, the one that would atomize economic power and economic influence. And we are also a long way from the Hayek view, that the market contains and distributes all the *useful* information. It now, increasingly, contains and distributes some *planted* information, which may not be objectively useful. So much for the dream of a completely free and libertarian market economy, one without controls that would promote freedom and social welfare for all.

The question of whether there is now a need to *control some aspects of the market*, or at least some attempts at distorting the market, as over the centuries, there had been the need of *controlling the power of the state or the government* (see Gordon, 1999) has become an increasingly relevant but, obviously, it remains a highly, controversial political question. It is clearly one that merits deep analysis by economists and social scientists.

The recent changes reported have also had an unavoidable impact on the fairness of the income distribution. Because of the changed policy and technological environment, in many cases, the same genuine effort by an individual, say a top athlete, an effort that in the distant past would have earned that individual a modest but fully deserved *income* has led to earnings that can be millions of US dollars, and to the inevitable questioning of the economic legitimacy of those earnings, especially by the many individuals who have continued to work hard but have continued to receive low or minimum wages that leave them and their families in relative poverty.

In a strictly economic sense, some of the new, inflated earnings could be considered mostly, or at least partly, undeserved "rents," rather than genuine "incomes," even when received from free market exchanges. This casts questions about the claimed fairness of the market economy as it is now working, the market that is supposed to make everyone equally free, and of the fairness of the income distribution that it creates. The creation of these rents had been helping especially a given category of economic agents and changing in their favor the income distribution.

Many workers have not benefited from these developments. Rather, they have been hurt by the globalization policies and, to some extent, by the increasing loss of jobs to automation. For them, the *rental* part of their total compensation has become zero, or at times even negative. This was not the way the capitalist system had been assumed to work. As it has been developing, that system has not been playing a neutral role in the distribution of income, and this has created some arguments in favor of the government to play some redistributive role, especially in some areas.

To repeat, the large change in compensation over the years for the same performance for some categories of individuals can be largely attributed to *public* policies.

Because of technological developments, such as the transistor, the Internet, and, for basic biological research, DNA and other advances in biology, it had become possible, for some clever and enterprising individuals and enterprises, to generate products and services that could be patented and sold to huge numbers of buyers.

Some of the sales, such as those of Twitter, are now made not directly to the ultimate users but to advertisers, who use the platforms to advertise various products and services, rather than compete by reducing the prices of the products and services they sell to the users. Today, drugs that require doctors' prescriptions, and even some hospital surgical procedures, are advertised directly to the patients, rather than to their doctors. Clearly this is not Adam Smith's, or Hayek's, or Stigler's market, and economists have been slow to recognize the changes that have taken place, and their importance for policies, in judging the ethics and also the efficiency of the market.

Some lucky individuals and enterprises can now extract huge profits that, because of complex tax laws, are effectively taxed at much lower rates than they should be or than they were in past decades. Some of the largest enterprises in the world today seem to have these intellectual–capital characteristics. They sell services that were initially made possible by the new knowledge provided by government-protected intellectual capital, and by the new associated knowledge, and sold at profits that are taxed at much lower rates than they would have been in past decades. In early 2020, one of these enterprises, Apple, became the largest enterprise in the whole world, in term of capitalization, taking the place that many years ago had been occupied by US Steel.

The world has really changed, and it has changed more than people may have realized! Unfortunately, for many it has not changed in a desirable way. Naturally, this raises the question of whether these enterprises and/or the high-income individuals should not share some of these gains with the society (national or even global) in which they live, either through higher taxes or through some other sharing arrangements, This might make it easier for governments to help the workers who have been the losers in these developments, and also by providing free, universal protection against risks that all individuals (rich and poor, and regardless of their racial or ethnic background) face, such as illnesses, low literacy, and old age, or through other arrangements that might be developed.

Artificial intelligence is likely to play an increasing but still uncertain role in future years. It will help humanity in some areas but, by making some or many workers unemployed, may leave them without an income, because of the impact of the automation of many tasks. It is an open question of where, or if, new jobs would be available for those who will lose their present jobs and where the aggregate demand will come from in a free market economy.

There is no question that new knowledge is needed to address some of the difficult issues that current developments have raised, as Keynes thought necessary in 1926, under different circumstances. As new illnesses require new drugs to deal with them, new social and economic developments are likely to require new policies and institutions. The latter can be seen as the needed drugs for social illnesses. It may be an illusion to believe that society and social arrangements need no changes, as conservatives continue to believe, and that the free market will continue to provide all the needed answers. It may or may not.

Another element of the change was the relatively novel view that financial incentives can have a great impact on the performance and on the productivity of some individuals, including, especially, of those who manage enterprises or money. Money compensation, and not duty, personal pride, reputation, or intellectual curiosity, was suggested to be the main driving force in many performances. The higher the money compensation promised or expected was, the better the personal performance would be. This provided a justification for some individuals in particular positions asking for higher compensation.

A related aspect of this view was that high taxes on these managers would negatively affect their incentives and reduce their performances, giving a justification for reducing tax rates. High taxes came to be seen as always bad, regardless of how the revenues were collected and how they were used by the government, and regardless of how high the gross compensations and how uneven the income distribution had become.

Strangely, the above view, that in recent decades played a major role in redistributing income toward a few individuals, was not assumed to apply to dependent workers but only to managers and to other independent performers, including individuals in the financial market, athletes, and artists. Therefore, the earnings of dependent workers could be constrained or squeezed as much as possible, to make possible the higher compensations for the few lucky ones (mostly managers, share owners, independent performers, and some others) who were expected to make the economy more efficient.

This view of personal behavior and performance in a capitalist system, a view that had not existed or had not been common in earlier decades (especially the period between 1940s and 1960s), made its strong appearance in the second half of the 1970s, and became prevalent in the United States in the 1980s. The tax related version of this view was reported to have made its first appearance in the form of a curve drawn on a restaurant napkin by an economist called Arthur Laffer and came to be called the "Laffer Curve."

The curve showed that a tax on personal income at a 0 or 100 percent rate would generate no revenue. As the rate fell from 100 percent, or rose above zero, the revenue to the government would increase, up to a maximum, at a relatively low rate. After that, the revenue would begin to fall because of the reactions of the taxed individuals to the higher rates, either by working less or by evading the taxes more.

Some interpretations of the Laffer Curve contributed to justify the asking for and the giving of what became absurdly large compensation packages, including huge bonuses and free company shares, given to CEOs and other managers, and to some other individuals in particular positions. Even managers of nonprofit organizations and of sport teams, and some university presidents, ended up getting million dollar compensations, presumably to make them more productive. That libertarian view has kept pushing for the further slashing of high marginal tax rates.

This thinking indirectly promoted and encouraged the squeezing of the wages of normal, dependent workers, a process that was facilitated by the ongoing globalization and by the accompanying weakening of the labor unions until recent years, a weakening that had started taking place in the late 1970s. For average workers, financial incentives, or higher wages, were not assumed to have any stimulating effect on their productivity; the stimulating effect was assumed to exist only for managers and for some other lucky individuals, not for workers.

It is not likely that Adam Smith, especially the Adam Smith of *The Theory of Moral Sentiments* (1759), would have endorsed these developments, attributed to the way capitalism should work and defended by many conservatives. Normal workers were reduced to robots. They were not supposed to respond to higher compensation, and statutory minimum wages continued to be kept low, and their existence was opposed by the managers of the enterprises and by conservative economists because they distorted the labor market.

The average compensation of corporate managers rose from the five times the average wages of workers that the first Nobel Prize Winner in Economics, Ian Tinbergen, had considered desirable in the 1950s, and from the about twenty times the level that had been assumed desirable by Peter Drucker, the famed, US management expert in the 1960s, to levels that, at times, have reached or exceeded 1,000 times the dependent workers' average wages. For example, today, the CEOs of Starbucks and of Chipotle, have been reported to earn 1,500 and 2,000 times, respectively, the average salaries of their workers. The CEO of Apple has been reported to receive about 1,500 times the compensation of the Apple dependents. On average, in the United States, managers now earn about 600 times the average wages of their workers. The growth rates of the economy in recent decades do not indicate that these compensations have had the expected impact on productivity.

Compensations in many millions or, at times, even in billions of dollars in the financial sector became more common and at times even expected and, again, these compensations are now far less taxed than they were half a century ago, in part because of the ways that the compensation packages are now structured, to take advantage of tax preferences that were introduced in recent decades for some kinds of compensations, such as "carried trade," delayed compensations that qualified as capital gain, and others, and in part because of the reduction in the tax rates since that took place since the 1980s.

There was no longer any embarrassment on the part of managers to ask for and to obtain huge compensations, from their often-docile corporate boards. On their side, the corporate boards did not want to be embarrassed by paying less to *their* managers than similar corporations were paying to *theirs*. Some managers got these high compensations even when the performances of the enterprises that they managed had been far from admirable.

This, for example, happened in Boeing, after two of its new, most advanced planes crashed within a few months, creating a major reputational crisis for that enterprise that much depended on its technical reputation. Not long after the crashes, the CEO of Boeing retired, but he still retired with tens of millions of dollars, presumably as compensation for his high productivity and good performance!

In the case of Boeing the close connection between the managers of the enterprise and the regulators seemed to have played an important role in allowing planes to fly with potential technical defects. It was an example of the Elite Network in action, in an area where it should not have been. The regulatory function of the government had been reduced or eliminated, in favor of self or no regulation. The complexity of modern technology and the unequal pay scales of government employees compared to that of the private sector may have created a situation where the regulators need the help of experts in the industry that they regulate to oversee the industry. As libertarians have continued to insist, the capitalist system will work best with no, or very few, regulations except self- regulation.

The experience in Boeing was far from rare. It had become increasingly common in the recent, market fundamentalist world which did not believe that regulations were useful but that, rather, they are harmful to the economy, by imposing unnecessary costs on enterprises.

In the financial market, some individuals have at times been awarded million dollars bonuses, also for good performances, just days before their institutions declared bankruptcy (see Stenfors, 2017, for examples). If the market is assumed to be always right, as it was supposed to be during the years of "market fundamentalism," and if its outcomes should not be questioned, these compensations were also not to be challenged. They should be assumed to have been fully deserved.

Another element of the perfect storm was the already reported major changes in the tax systems that occurred in many countries, and especially in the United States, in the 1980s onward. Further significant reductions

in taxes were introduced in 2017, by the Trump Administration, especially in taxes on corporate profits. In those years the high, marginal tax
rates on personal incomes, the ones that are especially important for the
highest incomes, were also dramatically reduced (in the United States
from 70 percent before 1980 to 28 percent in 1987) and taxes on corporations and on capital income were also slashed. These reductions had
been made in the belief that they would promote incentives and make the
economies more efficient.

The growing complexity in the tax systems, a complexity that has
increased over the years because of many micro changes in the laws or
changes in the interpretations of the existing laws, combined with the
effects of globalization on tax systems and of the new, intellectual services
that were traded, had created novel opportunities, for high net-worth
individuals and corporations, to shift profits to low tax jurisdictions, such
as Ireland, Luxembourg, and others, and to tax heavens, and thus to
evade, or avoid, many of the taxes that they should have paid.

Some of the most profitable corporations in the world today have been
reported to pay little taxes, as they had in the distant past. It has also been
estimated that the average tax rate on the incomes of billionaires is now
not much higher than that of average workers.

Other factors, such as deregulation, especially in the financial market;
the weakening of labor unions and some technological developments that
have made it easier for enterprises to replace workers with robots; globalization; and some others, have also played significant roles in changing
the social and economic landscape that existed five decades ago.

Clearly, the harmony that at least in part seemed to have existed or to
have been approached in the mid-1960s between the desired role of the
state and that of the market had been compromised, first by developments
in the late 1960s and 1970s and, more fundamentally, and later, by some
of the policies and views that market fundamentalism had brought in the
1980s onward.

Around 1995 there had been, again, the impression that prevailing
views and policies had converged, around a different and more libertarian
paradigm, one that seemed to have brought, once again, some harmony
between state and market. At that time the scope of the US welfare system
was modified and reduced by Clinton, a Democratic President. Requests
for a smaller government role had become popular. That harmony would
last a decade when new problems would appear to question it. Future
years would again be characterized by growing political and
social divisions.

A question that should be asked is whether a market economy, in countries that are still basically democratic and where most adult citizens can vote, can continue to retain its legitimacy and the real economic freedom of all its participants, when the income distribution becomes as uneven as it became in the United States in recent decades, and when it was creating a class of rich individuals (the Davos Guys? The Yachts Guys? The Venture Capitalists? The owners of the Media?) who, like the nobles of centuries ago, or the rich of the "Gilded Age" at the end of the nineteenth century in the United States, have enormous economic power, feel that they are different from the rest of the citizens, and believe that they are fully entitled to their wealth and, furthermore, that *their* wealth benefits everyone through trickle down.

Because of that wealth concentration, and because policies have become progressively more complex for the average voters to fully understand, the rich elites have more power to influence those who make the public policies by financing their political campaigns and activities, and to influence the voters by buying the major means of communications, such as newspapers. television stations, and enterprises such as Twitter, and controlling the news. We should ask whether this is the capitalist system that would make all of us free and more prosperous.

To some extent, but with significant differences, this was the situation that had existed in the advanced world in the 1920s, the decade before the Great Depression. That situation led to the changes in the decades that followed the Depression and the Second World War, until the 1970s. In 1926, Keynes had felt that the system that existed at that time could not continue as it was, and he had called for "new knowledge" to deal with the unsustainable situation and to make the necessary changes. Obviously, in his view, the laissez faire system then prevailing had not delivered what was needed (Keynes, 1926).

New knowledge appeared needed again after the financial difficulties and the Great Recession of 2007–2010, a knowledge that would suggest what should be done in the new circumstances. This knowledge should suggest some needed policy changes that would again bring more harmony between the economic role of the state, a role considered desirable by many, in a democratic society, and the economic results that the capitalist system as it is working, could deliver. Many observers do not consider the current results as satisfactory, especially on equity grounds, given the income distribution that now prevails.

In the view of many people, the needed harmony between role of state and that of the market does not exist today, especially in the United States and the United Kingdom. The growing societal divisions that exist in several advanced countries are clear indications of the absence of the needed harmony, and without that harmony the world risks moving again in unpredictable and not necessarily desirable directions, as it did in 1917 in Russia, and in some other places at different times.

Several political scientists have been expressing doubts that, in recent years, the world has been moving in the right direction. The future is beginning to look increasingly fragile for various reasons. See some reasons mentioned in Tanzi (2022).

The new harmony would need governments that are less exposed to lobbies; that use less-complex policies; that have the capacity to regulate efficiently and equitably the economy, without over-regulating or under-regulating, the work of the market; and that use policies that, while they retain the essential role of the market, in allocating resources and in maintaining some of the basic freedoms of individuals, make the sharing of the national pie more fair and more equitable than it has been in recent years.

The policies should reduce inequalities in the standard of living to a tolerable or acceptable level, but not reduce them to a level that would destroy legitimate economic incentives and personal freedom. We should want a compassionate capitalistic system, not a Marxist, centrally planned one. However, the habit of calling almost any government intervention "socialist," as some libertarians have continued to do, and opposing any tax increase, or any new regulation, does not help. It makes the problem worse.

Scandinavia and a few other countries, in recent years, have shown that a "third" or "intermediate" way may be possible, because money, while important, is not the only compass that guides, or should guide, the actions of humans in today's societies. Some "efficient inequality" in compensations and in the ownership of wealth, to compensate for significant, genuine differences in talent, efforts, and risk taking, must be retained. But too much inequality is not helpful, either to the economy or to society.

The basic goal should be the promotion of what could still be efficient markets; markets with some inevitable and necessary inequality in the distribution of incomes and wealth; and markets that would allow reasonable economic growth, in a setting considered fair and relatively free. That is, naturally, a tall order but an achievable one, as some countries have shown.

Remarkably, the Scandinavian countries and a few others have been performing close to the top, among advanced countries, in many of the relevant and comparable indices of economic performance even though they have high tax and high public spending levels. They have maintained remarkably low Gini coefficients for income, and much evidence indicates that they have managed to retain much individual freedom. Their labor participation is also very high. Perhaps other countries could learn from the Scandinavian countries' experience, unless the conclusion were that Scandinavian citizens are just from another planet, and that they respond to different incentives from those of other countries.

Of course, even in these countries there have been and there still are some who would prefer more libertarian policies and some who are not happy that immigrants can benefit from the welfare state's policies, even though they have not contributed to their financing. In these countries, and especially in Norway, some billionaires have chosen to move to countries, such as Switzerland, where taxes are lower. One could say that these few individuals have voted with their feet.

How much inequality would be required to keep economies efficient might be different among countries, depending on the culture, the history, and the community spirit of their members. Neither income equality, as centrally planned economies intended to achieve but never did, nor excessive income inequality, as the United States has now achieved, would be desirable. Community spirit deserves to be given more scope and more importance and to be promoted through education and in other ways. Economists have not helped by continually praising individualism, unrestrained economic freedom, and unrealistically low taxes.

In many countries and especially in the United States, tax policies and, perhaps, also spending programs, in recent decades, have not been in line with what was needed. The arguments about the economic inefficiency of high taxes, while they have some merit, were carried too far, while the arguments about "trickle down," from higher expected growth and from rich individuals, were too quickly believed, and were promoted by economists who should have known better.

There has also been the wrong perception that much public spending goes to lazy and underserving individuals. The fact that most of the amount goes to schools, defense, promotion of justice, police functions, public roads, and so on is generally ignored. Winning a Nobel Prize in Economics may have been an indication of technical skill by those who receive these prizes, but the prizes do not always necessarily indicate common wisdom on the part of those who receive them. Some leading economists, such as Hayek, have questioned the wisdom of giving such prizes. See, for example, the short speech that he gave in Stockholm at the banquet during his Nobel Prize, in *Essays on Hayek*, edited by Fritz Machlup (1976a, p. xviii).

The policy shortcomings in recent decades have not only been in tax and spending policies but also in monetary policy. Cheap money was promoted by the argument that it would stimulate employment and growth and that it would not have much effect on inflation, on income distribution, and on other government policies. Cheap money is likely to have done little to promote growth, while it may have become an important contributor to inequality, instability, and perhaps even to bad fiscal policy, by encouraging public borrowing over fair taxation.

Access to cheap money has not been the same for rich and poor individuals. This aspect has received little attention by relevant monetary economists. Monetary policy is likely to have contributed to future macroeconomic instability and to related problems, by encouraging the dependence of governments on public debts, in the expectation that real interest rates would remain low.

In 2022, inflation reappeared in a menacing manner, creating major challenges for the Federal Reserve Bank, for the ECB, and for other central banks on how to deal with it, and creating much uncertainty in the financial market. It forced the Federal Reserve, and later the ECB, to increases their rates. Inevitably, the stock market and the housing markets reacted. Fears of recession were again mentioned with increasing frequency. Good discussions of monetary policy in the United States in recent years, and of past mistakes, can be read in Leonard (2022) and de Larosière (2022).

23

More on Economy and Culture in the Present Time

Apart from the cultural and distributional changes, some reported earlier, there were other changes that came, especially in the 1980s onward. They were less directly connected with the behavior of CEOs and corporations and more with some of the undergoing cultural and economic developments. For example, consumers used less cash and more credit cards to make purchases; men wore less ties and more beards; and people held less cigarettes and more smart phones in their hands. The clothes that people wore were less refined and less influenced by fashion. Women showed more of their skin and some acquired tattoos. Not surprising, there were new drugs advertised that promised clearer skins for those who used them.

Another important change, noted by some observers, was the decline in the general etiquette and good manners that had characterized earlier periods. As the title of an article in the *Washington Post* of July 30, 2022, by Mitch Daniels, stated: "In a nasty era, insisting on politeness is a revolutionary idea." Daniels commented on the impact that this was having on public schools, which could no longer easily dismiss students for bad behavior, as they had done in the past. And there were more school and other senseless mass shootings, and even a shooting of a teacher by a six year old boy.

There was an important change in the pattern of spending to which we have already referred but that may be worth stressing. The spending that was directed toward items that could be bought in small, discrete, and variable quantities, such as food in food stores, and for which the economic law of demand clearly and directly applied, became less and less important in the total spending of individuals and families. The spending on items that were less subjected to the direct application of the law of demand (spending that had to be done in fixed amounts) became far more important. That spending included payment for property taxes, rents, various insurances, car purchases, fees for children's school tuition, payments for plane tickets, for club memberships, for medical expenses, for subscriptions to newspapers, and for many other purchases.

For many of the above expenditures the current and expected future family budget was important in determining what could be afforded or not and in what quality. But some flexibility in spending was lost, because the expenses could no longer be easily and quickly adjusted in a granular fashion, as it had been possible in the past, when income changed. This may have made real income reductions, during recessions or inflation, more painful and more difficult to cope with, especially for lower-income families that did not have accumulated wealth and already had high debts. The traditional law of demand, so important to economists, though still valid in general terms, through the price effect, became less directly applicable to the behavior of consumers than it had been in the past, in contrast with the income effect of many expenditures. "Tightening of the belt" became more difficult during income reductions because of fixed expenses.

By the beginning of the new century, some elements of the market economy had changed dramatically, in some countries more than in others. They seemed to have changed more in countries that had adopted policies of market fundamentalism and the changes had come in several areas.

An important structural change, that became increasingly pronounced, was the role that the use of new technologies and new intellectual capital, and of information in general, came to play in economic exchanges. Increasingly, the value of many of the exchanges came to depend more on their *intellectual and informational* content than on the value of the raw material and the basic labor input that had gone into them.

A very simple and clearly extreme example was that of cars. In the 1960s the cost of an average, American-made, car, say a Chevrolet, had been about one dollar per pound of weight. The weight of a car largely determined its cost. With all the electronics and the new technology that new cars now contain, this relationship has become meaningless, even when the dollar value is adjusted to reflect the inflationary changes.

An even more extreme example is that of smart phones. In the past phones were fixed and simple items that conveyed only the sound of the voices being spoken. Today, they have become encyclopedias, cameras, and much more. They provide users with a lot of useful information, including that conveyed by GPS, that can save users a lot of time and effort, in addition to weather forecasts, stock market results, and much else. In other words, they contain much information.

In recent decades an increasingly important role in exchanges has been played by the "publicness" of what is produced and sold, and by the role that the protection of intellectual capital plays or has played in determining the value of the exchange. Surprisingly, this aspect has not attracted as much attention as it may merit on the part of economists. For this reason, it may be worthwhile to allocate a bit of space to it.

Simply put, a lot of what had been mostly *private goods* in the past and their production became at least partly *public goods*. In a vague and not precise form, the concept of public good had been known to economists for a long time. Especially scholars of the Italian "Scienza delle Finanze," an important public finance "school" that had developed in Italy in the late nineteenth and early twentieth centuries, were aware of public goods that communities needed and that had to be provided by governments. It was believed that their provision required tax revenue. Generally, citizens wanted more public goods (more and better roads, more and better schools, police protection, etc.) but they did not like to pay the taxes that were needed to provide them. For libertarian individuals, this attitude does not seem to have changed. They have continued to complain of small portions, in some public goods, and high prices, in taxes.

Public goods started to attract more attention in the 1950s, at a time when economists were identifying new, theoretical justifications that could explain and justify the expansion of the role of the government in the economy that was taking place at that time. The new government role contrasted with the laissez faire policies of earlier years. Economists needed to justify the creation of the welfare states and why increases in tax burdens had become necessary. Many thought that the provision of public goods could not be left to the market, some public goods were clearly needed in growing economies, and governments had to be responsible for providing them.

Paul Samuelson had clarified the theoretical characteristics of pure public goods with his short, brilliant, and, later, much-cited article, published in 1954. He had identified the two fundamental characteristics that made a good *public*. The first was the possibility that adding more users to its consumption would not increase the cost of its provision. This characteristic came to be defined as the *jointness of supply*. The second was the inability, on the part of the provider of the public good, to prevent potential "free riders" from accessing and using it, once it had been produced, even if free riders had refused to contribute to the cost of its provision. This characteristic was defined as the *impossibility of exclusion*. It explained why the public good had to be provided by the state with public revenue, and not be left to the market.

The mechanical clocks on the bell towers in European towns (before the Industrial Revolution made cheap personal clocks available to many) had provided the time of the day to the town's citizens, were good examples of useful, pure public goods. Other examples were public monuments, beautiful cathedrals and churches, city walls, sidewalks, lighthouses, and others. Only the government, or some other clearly *public* institutions, including broadly based religious ones, when they acted for a whole community, might have an interest in providing these public good to the citizens, as they occasionally did in some European countries.

The mechanical clocks had added great value to the economy. They had made it possible for towns' citizens to know the time of the day, in order to arrange meetings and various schedules, to coordinate the opening and the closing of shops and working places, and to attend religious functions. The possibility of meeting these schedules became economically important, especially during the Industrial Revolution when working at home was replaced by working in large factories.

The Industrial Revolution had needed cheaper energy, but also knowledge of the time of day for workers. Without that knowledge the Industrial Revolution would have had a more difficult time. Both cheap energy and knowledge of time would play important roles in that Revolution. The workers needed to know the time of the day in order to report, in large numbers, to their work in the new factories. The city walls had provided protection to all the citizens of the cities from attacks from enemies. All these *public goods* needed public revenue to be provided. The higher the revenue, the more and the better public goods could be provided.

Private goods have characteristics that are symmetrically opposed to those of the public goods. They can be owned by single individuals and can be used only by those who own them. They can, thus, be bought and sold through the market, by private users and providers, and can be exchanged in private transactions. The market exists largely for this purpose. These goods are directly linked to the private market, and the government does not need to play a role in their exchanges or in their production, as Adam Smith had pointed out in *The Wealth of Nations* (1776).

In the distant past, at a time when the average incomes were much lower, much of what had been produced and exchanged, with few exceptions, had been "private goods." Once consumed by a person, or by a family, these goods were not available to anybody else. All foods seemed to satisfy that characteristic, and so did the clothes and the shoes that individuals wore. A piece of bread, an apple, or a fish, once eaten by a person was not available to other persons. A pair of shoes served only the person who was wearing them. These *private* goods constituted most of the consumption of individuals, and most of the production of the economy in the past. Market exchanges were mostly limited to these goods, and there were very few services exchanged in the market at that time. The few public goods provided by governments were limited by the available public resources, or occasionally they were provided by forced or slave labor.

As communities started to become more affluent, some goods appeared that began to have some limited characteristics of publicness, at least *over time*. Take, for example, books. In their hard copy, books are private goods when they are owned and are being read by the person who owns them. However, over time, they can be read by several persons, seriatim. Thus, over time, books can acquire some aspects of publicness. They can acquire even more publicness in modern audio versions that can be listened to by several individuals at the same time.

The publicness of books, over time, can explain the existence of public libraries, which already existed in antiquity. Rome was reported to have had forty public libraries. The same was true for horses, the services of which were strictly private, at one time, but they could be shared by more persons, over time, or when they pulled coaches that could carry several persons. Today this limited publicness has been extended to the use of cars (with taxis and Uber services) and even to houses, which their owners can rent to different persons at different times; or can own in time-sharing arrangements with others.

In the distant past, public spectacles were example of goods that had some characteristic of publicness. They could be enjoyed by many spectators at the same time, and additional "users" could be added, up to full capacity, at zero, or at low extra costs. Roman emperors made great use of these public spectacles, to sustain the support of Roman citizens, who much enjoyed them. Admission to these public spectacles could also be limited, at some low cost.

After the publication of Samuelson's two articles there were debates about what came to be called "quasi-public goods," goods such as roads, schools, or public hospitals, where additional users could be added, at least up to a point of congestion, and exclusion was technically possible, but at some costs that could be high. For some roads, toll roads could replace free roads, as Adam Smith had recommended, and toll roads could be provided by private interests, as had been done with turnpikes in England. But there would be costs in terms of equity in these exclusions, because only those who could afford to pay would be allowed to use them, as was the case with private goods. The pursuit of equity would have to be abandoned. Quasi-public goods became controversial as to the extent of the government obligation to provide some of them freely, at a time when equity was becoming a more important policy objective, and when welfare states were being created.

Quasi-public goods could be important parts of the packages that welfare states were offering to their citizens, because they could increase welfare and provide economic opportunities for low income individuals. For these reasons, some countries chose to provide these or some of the semi-public goods to all citizens, at no direct cost to the users. Some did not, or they restricted access to those goods to only limited categories of citizens. For these public goods, equity arguments were often important in the decisions, and they were controversial.

The more attention a country paid to equity and to creating equality of opportunities to all citizens, the more justification there was for providing some of these goods, such as education, health care, and some others, publicly and freely. The more were low incomes attributed to laziness or to other defects, the less justification there seemed to be to provide these quasi-public goods for free.

The provision of information created a different category of goods. It had potential jointness of consumption, but access to it could be restricted as it was for newspapers. Its availability could also be important in determining the distribution of income that a community would have. Naturally the value of information grows with the educational level of the population.

Let us now return to globalization and to its impact on economic activities. The process of deindustrialization, in recent decades in some advanced countries, that had accompanied the opening of national markets, was accompanied by a parallel process in which the production of goods with some characteristics of publicness replaced or accompanied, partly or largely, goods with clear characteristics of privateness. This process benefited workers who could provide the former while it hurt those who had been producing the latter in advanced countries. This inevitably had an impact on the income distribution within countries. In the United States it led to the deindustrialization of some areas, and many industrial workers lost out, while more educated workers who were associated with the production of the new electronically based goods, many in Silicon Valley in California and in other important hubs, gained.

This chapter has reported on some changes that took place in attitudes and in economic relations in recent decades, starting in the 1970s. There is no question that today's world is different in important ways from the world that had existed in the 1970s, and this is not just because the average income that people enjoy has gone up. There were other important changes that took place.

Before closing this chapter, it may be worthwhile to mention another more recent change that is becoming progressively more apparent but that is outside the scope of this book, because its longer-term impact on culture and income distribution is not easily predictable at this time, to allow some significant analysis. We shall limit ourselves to mentioning that change without any elaboration.

While in the 1970s and later years the process of globalization had generally been endorsed by most economists, because it was the old Ricardian one of making the available productive resources of the whole world more efficient, by opening frontiers, by removing trade restrictions, and by encouraging higher global productivity, in the most recent years that goal seems to have changed for at least two main reasons.

First, this goal has been replaced by that of pursuing what have become more strictly *national*, rather than *global*, objectives. This has happened especially, but not only, in the two largest world economies, the United States and China. Increasingly, these countries have replaced the earlier *global* goal with more *nationalist* goals. They have done so by introducing various obstacles to free trade, and especially by providing assistance to some national activities.

Secondly, some critical technologies have become increasingly important in the production of some outputs that have become more important in some activities. These outputs require great sophistication to produce and they require access to some rare materials that only a few countries are capable of producing. This change has been brought about by the progressive switch that had been taking place over the years from the importance and the use in production of steel and more easily and broadly available raw materials, to that of rare natural materials ("rare earths") that have become increasingly essential in producing chips or semiconductors, which are critical in many modern outputs.

The production of chips and other inputs, into products such as advanced batteries and many others, require very sophisticated technical knowledge and very costly machines that are available in only a few countries and in a few enterprises. These are available in only a few places. These factors have changed the nature of globalization. As a well-informed author has put it:

Once the chip industry took shape it proved difficult to dislodge it from Silicon Valley. Today's semiconductor supply chain requires components from many cities and countries. But almost every chip made still has a Silicon Valley connection or is produced with tools designed and built in California. America's vast reserve of scientific expertise nurtured by government research funding and strengthened by the ability to poach the best scientists from other countries has provided the core knowledge driving technological advances forward.

(Miller, 2022,p. xxii)

Semiconductors are now essential for many new modern products, and they are likely to become even more so in years to come, stimulating strong competition among countries and promoting new "industrial policies.". The loser may be the goal of globalization with fair competition, and perhaps even some of the new technologically-based enterprises born in the 1980s and 1990s. The full application of Artificial Intelligence is still in its infancy as the battle for Internet search has recently demonstrated. Microsoft has integrated ChatDPT into its search engine, Bing, perhaps, ending the monopoly that Google has had so far in search engines. Artificial Intelligence may bring many surprises in the future.

24

Some Summing Up and Concluding Observations

This book has aimed at providing a broad and historically based review of economic developments, of social attitudes, and of policies over the past two centuries, with special attention to the United States, and with much of the focus on the period after the Second World War. It has outlined views and changes in views that took place about the importance of equity and of income distribution in economic policy and outcomes, that economists and other intellectuals have held over the years. It has highlighted and criticized the excessive focus that economists gave to the concept of economic efficiency, combined with their relative indifference toward the distribution of income and wealth or, more generally, toward equity.

The prevailing view by economists was that promoting efficiency was enough to promote communities' welfare and that economists lacked the scientific tools to make judgments about desirable income distribution. This book has considered that position naïve and even dangerous, especially when income distributions become very uneven, as they have done in recent decades, and when they prevail for long periods, creating not only economic but also social and class differences. Higher incomes and wealth, and the economic and political power that accompanies them when they are maintained over the longer term, sooner or later come to be seen as entitlements on the part of those who are benefitting from them. This inevitably changes the true meaning of democracy.

The book has stressed that, when the goal of equity is ignored by the economic policies pursued by the government, and also by the market, and when the income distribution becomes increasingly uneven, sooner or later there will be popular reactions from those left at the lower end of the income distribution, especially but not only in countries that are still democratic and where many continue to have the power to vote.

The likelihood of these popular reactions had been recognized in the distant past, not only by socialist economists, such as Karl Marx and others, but also by important mainstream economists, such as Edwin Seligman, a prominent professor at Columbia University in the early part of the twentieth century. Very uneven income distributions are likely to provoke populist reactions and, at times, to lead to revolutions or, at least, to sharply new and different policies, which may not be market oriented and may damage the essential role that the market should play in allocating resources.

Libertarian and laissez faire economists created a mythology that connected general economic performance to the financial gains for what could be relatively small groups of individuals, the winners (see Oreskes and Conway, 2023). The fact that the total output was unevenly distributed did not matter for them. What mattered was the growth of national output. Total or national output and its growth have remained the most important guiding indicators for many economists until today. Low taxes and low tax rates became important elements of that mythology. The enormous compensations of managers and of some other economic agents were important aspects of it.

While there is no question that *some* incentives given to *more talented, more risk taking,* and *harder working* individuals are necessary and are helpful in keeping an economy efficient and productive, excessive financial compensations, that lead to much less even income distributions but often generate little additional productivity, are likely to lead to reactions by those at the lower end of the distribution and, in the longer term, are likely to become counterproductive and create problems.

Some countries, including the Scandinavian countries and a few others, have shown that a "third" or intermediate "way" is possible, paying relatively minor efficiency costs. They have shown that *sufficient* incentives can coexist with an appreciation of the goal of respecting some equity objectives for whole communities. It is not necessary to choose between extreme alternatives, or "corner solutions." As is the case in many life situations, the middle ground may, and often does, offer preferable and sustainable alternatives.

The obsession with the pursuit of efficiency in economic policies and economic growth that has characterized the market fundamentalist policies of the 1980s and 1990s, first, did not seem to have delivered the large gains that it had promised in terms of economic growth and, second, had sharply negative impacts on some workers and especially on many industrial workers, who were damaged by the policies adopted and were told to take care of themselves because the government would not help them. The view was that the free market would somehow deal with the transition, a view that turned out to be unrealistic and wrong.

There has been a continuing dream on the part of some economists, that an economy driven by conservative or libertarian principles, one with *very* low taxes and *very* few regulations on economic operators and citizens, would somehow preserve the freedom of *all* individuals and make countries prosperous and communities happy. An almost Pavlovian reaction developed among some groups in favor of what are broadly defined as libertarian principles.

The problem is that these libertarian principles are advocated *in principle*. They are never spelled out in detail. One is left to guess what they would be, in the real and highly urbanized world of today, and not in the abstract world of theory, or in the rural world of a distant past, when laissez faire had first been advocated. How far would libertarians go in reducing or eliminating taxes and regulations in today's world? One is left guessing and wondering.

We do know that some rules are *always* needed. Just think of traffic rules in crowded cities. And we know that *some* public revenues are *always* necessary, both to enforce the rules that exist and to provide public goods and services that are essential to a modern economy and community, including national defense and increasingly environmental protection. These needs have become especially important in today's urban and industrial societies, in which most people no longer live in distant and isolated rural settings, where they could generate little negative externalities, and where they needed little public goods.

In modern societies negative externalities have become common, and very unequal standards of living have created problems (such as more crimes, poor health, homeless people, and others) and more unhappiness and resentments among many of those at the bottom, which are often the majority. These resentments can be considered *negative forms of externalities of a psychological character*.

We do not know how a truly libertarian economy would work in a *modern* economy, an economy with industrial activities and with populations with higher average incomes, that live in large and congested cities, and that can and do generate many negative externalities. These economies are different from the rural ones that existed when laissez faire policies were first advocated, and when they were favored, over the likely "mercantilist" policies that governments had been following, in countries that were, then, much less democratic.

From the more libertarian experience of the 1980s and 1990s, especially in the United States and the United Kingdom, we know that public spending did not go down much, and neither did the average tax *levels*, as distinguished from what happened to the *marginal tax rates* on high incomes and taxes on corporate profits, that were sharply reduced. What changed was the distribution of the tax burden and that of income in favor of those with high incomes.

Many rules were removed in those years, but many remained, and some new rules were added. The removal of some rules would also lead to new problems in the later years, as happened to the housing market and other areas.

What to do with the specific rules and with the tax levels and tax rates requires careful thinking and not general, a priori, libertarian wishes, which may lead to bad policies. For example, even convinced libertarians would not wish to allow drivers to drive at any speed in crowded cities, or to allow them to drive while intoxicated. They would not wish people to throw the garbage that they produce in the street or to make excessive noise. To believe that, without rules, free individuals would behave responsibly and not generate negative externalities and other problems is simply wishful thinking.

Whether libertarian or not, countries would need roads to accommodate cars, pedestrians, bicyclists, and others, and tax revenue to build and maintain roads and public schools. They would also need rules (and public revenue) to regulate traffic and reduce accidents. In the United States there were far more accidents when cars were first introduced and when there were still no rules to regulate traffic.

Countries would need rules that promote hygienic behavior by the population, to prevent the spread of infectious illnesses, illnesses that were frequent during laissez faire times, when fewer such rules existed. They would need rules to protect the environment and to deal with climate change. And they would need money for national defense, for police protection, for justice, for public schools, for jails, and for other public needs and functions. To finance these *public* activities, they would need tax revenues; and to regulate and enforce the existing rules they would need trained personnel and more public spending.

Especially modern, urbanized, and more mobile industrial countries, that burn much coal, oil, and gas, and that generate much garbage, including plastic and dangerous substances, and that warm and cool residences and other buildings using dirty fuels, create environmental problems that do not have political affiliations. Those problems do not disappear in libertarian countries. The latter would still need to regulate the relevant activities and to collect the tax revenue needed to finance their governments.

Global warming is no longer a vague and distant danger. It has become a worrisome and costly current reality. Specific policies are needed to deal with its dangerous consequences (see Tanzi, 2022). Appeals to vague, libertarian principles do not change this reality.

The debate should be on the concrete details of what to do, and on how to do it most efficiently, and not on vague principles. Hiding behind vague principles is not helpful, it just promotes friction and controversy, delays needed solutions, and puts the future at risk. It distorts the political debate from where it should be: from how to efficiently use the available public (and private) resources to deal with real problems.

Countries do not live in a totally peaceful world, and wars occasionally remind us of the need to keep strong military defenses, as the recent war in Ukraine has done. Military costs can be high and, somehow, they need to be covered by taxes, even in libertarian states. Should the debate not be on who benefits the most from defense spending, and who should contribute more to its financing rather than on the possibly negative efficiency impact of taxes and public spending?

How should the needed tax burden be distributed among the citizens, in countries with high income concentrations? Should "ability to pay" still be a valid principle of taxation, or was that principle made irrelevant by the Laffer Curve? Are "tax expenditures," in place of public spending programs, desirable? Are flat taxes good and realistic alternatives to taxes based on the ability to pay, especially in countries with highly uneven income distributions? Are flat taxes desirable in countries with very high Gini coefficients? Even if one favored more flat taxes, the existing "tax expenditures" would need to be eliminated to broaden the tax base before the taxes were applied. How realistic would such a policy be in countries which have already introduced hundreds of tax expenditures, as has the United States?

Countries with more educated populations do better in the modern, competitive world. If the government does not provide free educational services to the citizens, many individuals would remain uneducated, or would be much less educated, with all the economic and social consequences that follow from that. Governments will naturally need public resources to allow *all* children to get at least a minimum education and to allow some of the more talented but poorer students to obtain higher educational levels. Once again, the government will need public resources to do so.

All the above indicate that the Libertarian Emperor, as he is often presented, has got no clothes on and it would be better if he wore some. Libertarian economists should have the wisdom and the courage to recognize that truth and deal with it. This, of course, does not mean, and should not be interpreted to conclude, that everything governments do today is necessary, is productive, and is useful. Or that it is done in the most efficient way. There are activities that would better be left to the market, if this did not overly damage the equity objective. And there is obviously waste in some of the government operations and programs, so that the fight against waste should be and should remain important.

Some taxes are collected because of unproductive or unnecessary government expenses, as there were many such expenses during the fight against COVID-19, and corruption is often present within sone of the activities of the public sector. There are some regulations that were sponsored by groups in the private sector, to help them get some rents. Some public expenses have been pushed higher by private sector's interests. Ceteris paribus, efficient but necessary government activities would need less tax revenue and less public debt. But they would still need far more revenue and more rules than libertarian economists imagine or believe possible.

This all suggests that the debate should be directed at keeping the government role as slim and as efficient as possible, while respecting equity objectives, both in relation to public spending and to regulations and taxes. It should not ignore equity objectives or the existence of negative externalities.

The debate should not be the unfocused one, against the government and against taxes and regulations, that libertarians and conservatives often conduct. It should be a continuous debate on *specific* actions and policies. This would give it focus and make it a useful one. It would be a debate that would lead to better policies and to more efficient governments and markets, and to higher welfare for most.

It ought to be possible, for competent economists and public administrators, to determine the most efficient ways to meet and to finance needed public expenses (defense, education, roads, internal safety, justice, essential safety nets, regulations, and so on), rather that attacking governmental actions in the abstract, including the collection of taxes. The tax administration should be an example of efficiency rather than have its resources cut. By focusing on each major activity that the government engages in, it should be possible to determine the most efficient and cheapest way of achieving that activity.

This exercise would give us some estimates of the total tax revenue that would be necessary to deliver the *needed* package by an *efficient* government. This would shift the debate on the best way to collect the needed taxes without illusions, and on the best way to deliver essential government services. Such an exercise would give the public debate a focused and scientific base, a focus that it has badly lacked so far.

There would still be debate and controversy on some borderline expenditure, and on some aspects of the tax structure, but it would be on specific practical issues rather than on abstract or ideological principles. We may discover that the issues are fewer than many had believed, and that the needed tax levels are higher than libertarians think that they should be. With this experiment and exercise, the libertarian emperor would finally appear in public with some needed and dignified clothes, rather than continue to go around indecently naked.

References

Adams, Charles, 1998, *Those Dirty Rotten Taxes: The Tax Revolts that Built America* (New York: Free Press).

Agrawal, Ajay, Joshua Gans, and Avi Goldfarb, 2018, *Prediction Machines: The Simple Economics of Artificial Intelligence* (Cambridge, MA: Harvard Business School Press).

Akerlof, George A., 1970, "The Market for 'Lemons': Quality, Uncertainty and the Market Mechanism." *Quarterly Journal of Economics*, 84:3, 488–500.

Ambrose, Stephen, 2000, *Nothing Like It in the World: The Men who Built the Transcontinental Railroad 1863–1869* (New York: Simon & Schuster).

Ariely, Dan, 2008, *Predictably Irrational: The Hidden Forces that Shape Our Decisions* (New York: Harper Collins Publishers).

Arrow, Kenneth, 1951, *Social Choice and Individual Values* (New York: John Wiley & Sons).

Ashton, T. S., 1948, *The Industrial Revolution 1760–1830* (Oxford: Oxford University Press).

Atkinson, A. B. and Gunnar Viby Mogensen, eds., 1993, *Welfare and Work Incentives; A North European Perspective* (Oxford: Clarendon Press).

Barone, Enrico, [1907] 1935, "The Ministry of Production in the Collectivist State," in *Collectivist Economic Planning*, edited by Friedrich A. Hayek (London: Routledge and Kegan Paul), pp. 245–290.

Bastiat, F., 1864, *Oevres Completes*, 7 Vols. (Paris: Guillaimines).

Bator, Francis M, 1958, "The Anatomy of Market Failure." *The Quarterly Journal of Economics*, 72:1, 351–379.

Bernanke, Ben S., 2022, *21st Century Monetary Policy: The Federal Reserve from the Great Inflation to Covid-19* (New York: W. W. Norton and Company).

Bhagwati, Jagdish, 2004, *In Defense of Globalisation* (New York: Oxford University Press).

Blair, Linda, 2012, *The Washington Post*, May 12, p. A11.

Blinder, Alan S., 2013, *After the Music Stopped: The Financial Crisis, the Response, and the Work After* (New York: Penguin Press).

Bluestone, Barry and Bennett Harrison, 1982, *The Deindustrialization of America: Plant Closing, Community Abandonment and the Dismantling of Basic Industry* (New York: Basic Books).

Briody, Dan, 2003, *The Iron Triangle: Inside the Secret World of the Carlyle Group* (New York: John Wiley and Sons).

Brynjolfsson, Erik and Andrew McAfee, 2014, *The Second Machine Age: Work, Progress, and Prosperity in a time of Brilliant Technologies* (New York: W. W Norton and Company).

Buchan, James, 2006, *The Authentic Adam Smith* (New York: W. W. Norton and Company).

Buchanan, James. 1975, *The Limits of Liberty: Between Anarchy and Leviathan* (Chicago: University of Chicago Press).

Buchanan, James and Richard A. Musgrave, with an Introduction by Hand-Werner Sinn, 1999, *Public Finance and Public Choice: Two Contrasting Visions of the State* (Cambridge, MA: MIT Press).

Burtless, Gary, 2014, "Has Rising Inequality Brought Us Back to the 1920s? It Depends on How We Measure Income," *Brookings*, Upfront, May 20.

Carson, Rachel, 1962, *Silent Spring* (Boston: Houghton Mifflin).

Chetty, Raj, Nathaniel Herdren, Patrick Kline, Emmanuel Saez, and Nicholas Turner, 2014, "Is the United States a Land of Opportunity? Recent Trends on Intergenerational Mobility," Working Paper 19844. NBER, January.

Cornes, Richard and Todd Sandler, 1986, *The Theory of Externalities, Public Goods and Club Goods* (Cambridge: Cambridge University Press).

Diamond, Peter and Emmanuel Saez, 2011, "The Case for a Progressive Tax: From Basic Research to Policy Recommendations." *Journal of Economic Perspectives*, 25:4, 165–190.

Diner, Steven J., 1998, *A Very Different Age: Americans of the Progressive Era* (New York: Hill and Wang).

Domitrovic, Brian, 2010, "Economic Policy and the Road to Serfdom: The Watershed of 1913," in *Back on the Road to Serfdom: The Resurgence of Statism*, edited by Thomas Woods Jr. (Wilmington, DE: ISI Books).

Faulkner, Harold U., 1951, *The Decline of Laissez Faire, 1897–1917*, Vol. VII, The Economic History of the United States (White Plains, NY: M. E. Sharpe Inc.).

Fogel, Robert William, 2000, *The Fourth Great Awakening and the Future of Egalitarianism* (Chicago: The University of Chicago Press).

Frank, Robert H., 2005, "The Mysterious Disappearance of James Duesenberry," *The New York Times*, June 9.

Friedman, Benjamin, 2021, *Religion and the Rise of Capitalism* (New York: Alfred A. Knopf).

Friedman, Milton, 1963, *Capitalism and Freedom* (Chicago: University of Chicago Press).

1970, "The Social Responsibility of Business Is to Increase Its Profits." *New York Times Magazine*, September 21.

Gelles, Davis, 2022, *The Man Who Broke Capitalism* (New York: Simon & Schuster).

George, Henry, 1879, *Progress and Poverty* (New York: D. Appleton and Company).

Giddens, Anthony, 1998, *The Third Way: The Renewal of Social Democracy* (Cambridge, UK: Polity Press).

Gilens, Martin, 2014, *Why Americans Hate Welfare* (Chicago: Chicago University Press).

Glantz, Aaron, 2019, *Homewreckers* (New York: Harper Collins Books).

Goodman, Peter, 2022, "C.E.O.s Were Our Heroes ... At Least According to Them." The New York Times, Sunday Business, January 16, p. 1 and 5.

Gordon, Scott, 1999, *Controlling the State: Constitutionalism from Ancient Athens to Today* (Cambridge, MA: Harvard university Press).

Greenspan, Alan, 2007, *The Age of Turbulence: Adventure in a New World* (New York: Penguin Press).

Gravelle, Jane G., 1986, "International Tax Competition: Does It Make a Difference for Tax Policy?" *National Tax Journal*, 39:3, 375–386.

Hayek, F. A., 1960, *The Constitution of Liberty* (Chicago: University of Chicago Press).

[1944] 2007, *The Road to Serfdom*, edited by Bruce Caldwell (Chicago: University of Chicago Press).

Head, John G., 1974, *Public Goods and Public Welfare* (Durham, NC: Duke University Press).

Hemel, Daniel, 2022, "The American Retirement System Is Built for the Rich." The Washington Post, Outlook, April 24, p. 1 and 4.

Hill, Fiona, 2021, *There is Nothing for You Here* (New York: Harper Collins Publishers).

Johnson, Harry G. 1973, "Some Micro Economic Reflections on Income and Wealth Inequality." *Annals of the American Academy of Political and Social Science*, 409, 53–60.

de Jouvenel, Bertrand, 1952, *The Ethics of Redistribution* (Indianapolis: Liberty Press).

Keynes, John Maynard, 1920, *The Economic Consequences of The Peace* (Mineola, NY: Dover Publications Inc.).

1926, *The End of Laissez Faire* (London: Hogarth Press).

Khaled, Abdel-Kader, and Ruud De Mooij, 2000, "Tax Policy and Inclusive Growth." IMF Working Paper, QP/29/271.

Klein, Lawrance R., 1947, *The Keynesian Revolution* (New York: The Macmillan Company).

Knight, Frank, [1921] 1964, *Uncertainty and Profit* (New York: Century Press).

Knowles, Caroline, 2022, *Serious Money: Walking Plutocratic London* (London: Allen Lane).

Kolata, Gina and Benjamin Mueller, 2022, "Decades of Discoveries Before 'Miraculous' Sprint of Vaccine." *The New York Times*, January 16, p. 1 and 13.

Kornai, Janos, 1992, *The Socialist System: The Political Economy of Communism* (Princeton: Princeton University Press).

Krugman, Paul, 1994, *The Age of Diminishing Expectations* (Cambridge, MA: MIT Press).

Lacey, A. R., 2001, *Robert Nozick* (Princeton: Princeton University Press).

Lange, Oskar and Fred M. Taylor, 1938, *On the Economic Theory of Socialism* (New York: McGraw-Hill).

de Larosière, Jacques, 2022, *Putting an End to Financial Illusions* (Paris: Odile).

LeGrand, Julian, 1991, *Equity and Choice: An Essay in Economics and Applied Philosophy* (London: Harper Collins Academic).

Leonard, Christopher, 2022, *The Lords of Easy Money: How the Federal Reserve Broke the American Economy* (New York: Simon & Schuster).

Leroy-Beaulieu, Paul, 1888, *Traite' de la Science des Finances* (Paris: Guillaumin).

Locke, John, [1690?] 1939, *Treatise of Civil Government and a Letter Concerning Toleration*, edited by Charles L. Sherman (Indianapolis: Appleton Century Crifts).

Loria, Achille, 1903, *Il Movimento Operaio* (Milan: Remo Sandron, Editore).

Lowenstein, Roger, 2022, *Ways and Means: Lincoln and His Cabinet and the Financing of the Civil War* (New York: Penguin Press).

MacLean, Nancy, 2017, *Democracy in Chains: The Deep History of the Radical Right's Stealth Plan for America* (New York: Viking).

Machlup, Fritz, ed., 1976a, *Essays on Hayek* (New York: New York University Press).

    1976b, "Hayek's Contribution to Economics," in *Essays on Hayek*, edited by Fritz Machlup (New York: New York University Press).

Mallock, W. H., 1908, *A Critical Examination of Socialism* (London: John Murray).

Marquez, Patricio V., 2023, "Tobacco Use, 'Deaths of Despair,' and Widening Inequality in Life Expectancy in the United States," February 1, available at: www.pvmarquez.com/lifeexpectancydropinUS

Marx, Karl, [1867] 1906, *Capital: A Critique of Political Economy* (New York: The Modern Library, Random House Inc.).

Marx, Karl and Friedrich Engels, 1948, *The Communist Manifesto* (London).

Messere, Ken, 1993, *Tax Policy in OECD Countries: Choice and Conflicts* (Amsterdam: IBFD Publications BV).

Milanovic, Branko, 2016, *Global Inequality: A New Approach for the Age of Globalization* (Cambridge, MA: Belknap Harvard).

Mill, John Stuart, [Various Years] 1962, *Utilitarianism, on Liberty, Essay on Bentham* (New York: New American Library).

    [1848] 2004, *Principles of Political Economy* (Amherst, NY: Prometheus Books).

Miller, Chris, 2022, *Chip War: The Fight for the World's Most Critical Technology* (New York: Scribner)

Miller, Eugene F., 2010, *Hayek's Constitution of Liberty* (London: The Institute of Economic Affairs).

Mitchell, Lawrence E., 2007, *The Speculation Economy: How Finance Triumphed over Industry* (San Francisco: Berret-Koehler).

Mokyr, Joel, 1990, *The Lever of Riches: Technological Creativity and Economic Progress* (New York: Oxford University Press).

Morris, Charles R., 2008, *The Two Trillion Dollar Meltdown: Easy Money, High Rollers* (New York: Public Affairs).

Mosher, Frederick C. and Orville F. Poland, 1964, *The Costs of American Government: Facts, Trends and Myths* (New York: Dodd, Mead and Company).

Mueller, Dennis C., 1989, *Public Choice II* (Cambridge: Cambridge University Press).

Muller, Jerry Z., 1993, *Adam Smith in His Time and Ours: Designing the Decent Society* (New York: Free Press).

Nozick, Robert, 1974, *Anarchy, State, and Utopia* (New York: Basic Books).

Okrent, Daniel, 2019, *The Guarded Gates: Bigotry, Eugenics, and the Law that Kept Two Generations of Jews, Italians and Other Europeans Immigrants out of America* (New York: Scribner).

Olson, Mancur Jr., 1969, *The Logic of Collective Action: Public Goods and the Theory of Groups* (New York: Schocken Books).

Oreskes, Naomi and Erik M. Conway, 2023, *The Big Myth: How American Business Taught Us to Loathe Government and Love the Free Market* (New York: Bloomsbury Publishers).

Palley, Thomas I., 2008, "The Relative Income Theory of Consumption: A Synthetic Keynes-Duesenberry-Friedman Model." University of Massachusetts Amherst, Political Economy Research Institute, Working Paper Series. N. 170.

Pechman, Joseph A., 1987, *Federal Tax Policy*, 5th ed. (Washington, DC: The Brookings Institution).

Pigou, A. C., 1920, *The Economics of Welfare* (London: MacMillan).

Piketty, Thomas, Emmanuel Saez, and Stefanie Stantcheva, 2014, "Optimal Taxation of Top Labor Incomes: A Tale of Three Elasticities." *American Economic Journal: Economic Policy*, 6:1, 230–271.

Piketty, Thomas, Emmanuel Saez, and Gabriel Zucman, 2018, "Distributional National Accounts: Methods and Estimates for the United States." *The Quarterly Journal of Economics*, 133:2, 553–609.

Pipes, Richard, 1999, *Property and Freedom* (New York: Alfred A. Knopt).

Polackova-Brixi, Hana and Allen Schick, eds., 2002, *Government at Risk: Contingent Liabilities and Fiscal Risk* (Washington, DC: World Bank).

Porter, Glenn, 1992, *The Rise of Big Business, 1850–1920* (Arlington Heights, IL: Harlan Davidson Inc.).

Puviani, Amilcare, [1903] 1973, *Teoria dell' Illusione Finanziaria*, edited by Franco Volpi (Milan: ISEDI).

Rajan, Raghuram G., 2010, *Fault Lines* (Princeton: Princeton University Press).

Rawls, John, 1971, *A Theory of Justice* (Cambridge, MA: Belknap Press).

1993, *Political Liberalism* (New York: Columbia University Press).

Reid, T. R., 2017, *A Fine Mess: A Global Quest for Simpler, Fairer, and More Efficient Tax Systems* (New York: Penguin Press).

Ricardo, David, 1817, *On the Principles of Political Economy and Taxation* (London: John Murray).

Ropke, Wilhelm, 1969, *Against the Tide* (Chicago: Henry Regnery Company).

2006, *Il Vangelo non e' socialista: Scritti su etica Cristiana e liberta' economica, a cura di Carlo Lottieri* (Italy: Rubettino Leonardo Facco).

Saez, Emmanuel and Gabriel Zucman, 2019, *The Triumph of Injustice: How the Rich Dodge Taxes and How to Make Them Pay* (New York: W. W. Norton and Company).

Samuelson, Paul, 1954, "The Pure Theory of Public Expenditure." *Review of Economics and Statistics*, 37, 350–356.

Sandel, Michael, J., 2012, *What Money Can't Buy: The Moral Limits of Markets* (New York: Farrar, Straus and Giroux).

Scherer, Michael and Sarah Ellison, 2022, "How a Billionaires Boys' Club Came to Dominate the Public Square." *The Washington Post*, May 1, p. 1, 4.

Scheidel, Walter, 2017, *The Great Leveler: Violence and the History of Inequality from the Stone Age to the Twenty-First Century* (Princeton: Princeton University Press).

Schlesinger, Arthur M., Jr., 1959, *The Coming of the New Deal* (Boston: Houghton Mifflin Company).

1960, *The Politics of Upheaval: 1935–1936* (Boston: Mariner Books).

Schuknecht, Ludger, 2020, *Public Spending and the Role of the State* (Cambridge: Cambridge University Press).

Schumpeter, Joseph A., [1942] 1950, *Capitalism, Socialism and Democracy*, 3rd ed. (New York: Harper and Brothers).

1954, *History of Economic Analysis* (New York: Oxford University Press).

Schwartzman, Paul, 2022, "In Laffer's Eyes, His Views Are Still Ahead of the Curve." *The Washington Post*, November 4, Style Section, p. 1 and 3.

Self, Peter, 1993, *Government by the Market? The Politics of Public Choice* (Boulder: Westview Press).

Seligman, Edwin R. A., 1907, *The Economic Interpretation of History*, 2nd ed. (New York: Columbia University Press).

Seligman, E. R. A., and Scott Nearing, 1922, *Capitalism Versus Socialism, A Public Debate* (New York: The Fine Arts Guild).

Serra, Antonio, 1613, *Breve Trattato delle Cause che Possono far Abbondare l'Oro e l'Argento dove non ci sono Miniere* (Naples: Lazzaro Scoriggio).

Shiller, Robert J., *Irrational Exuberance* (New York: Barnes and Nobles).

2012, *Finance and the Good Society* (Princeton: Princeton University Press).

Shome, Partho, ed., 2022, *Prevailing and Emerging Dilemmas in International Taxation, International Tax Research and Analysis Foundation (ITRAF)* (Bangalore: OakBridge).

Sinn, Hans-Werner, 2010, *Casino Capitalism: How the Financial Crisis Came about and What Needs to be Done Now* (Oxford: Oxford University Press).

Smith, Adam, 1759, *The Theory of Moral Sentiments* (London: Andrew Millar).

1776, *The Wealth of Nations* (London: W. Strahan and T. Cadell).

Smith, Vernon L., 2008, *Rationality in Economics* (Cambridge: Cambridge University Press).

Solimano, Andres, 2012, *Capitalismo a la Cilena: y la Prosperidas de las Elites* (Santiago: Editorial Catalonia).

2014, *Economic Elites, Crises and Democracies* (Oxford: Oxford University Press).

2020, *A History of Big Recessions in tong Twentieth Century* (Cambridge: Cambridge University Press).

Solomon, Howard M., 1972, *Public Welfare, Science and Propaganda in 17th-Century France: The Innovations of Theophraste Renaudot* (Princeton: Princeton University Press).

Solow, Robert M., 2005, "How Did Economics Get This Way and What Way Did It Get?" *Daedalus*, 126:1, 39–58.

Spenser, Herbert, 1884, *The Man Versus the State* (Indianapolis: Appleton).

Stenfors, Alexis, 2017, *Barometer of Fear: An insider's Account of Rogue Trading and the Greatest Banking Scandal in History* (London: Zen Books).

Steuerle, C. Eugene, 1992, *The Tax Decade: How Taxes Came to Dominate the Public Agenda* (Washington: The Urban Institute).

Stigler, George J., 1975, *The Citizen and the State: Essays on Regulation* (Chicago: University of Chicago Press).

Stiglitz, Joseph, 2003, *Globalization and Its Discontents* (New York: W. W. Norton).

Summers, Lawrence H., 2013, "Economic Possibilities for Our Children." NBER no. 4.

Surrey, Stanley, 1973, *Pathway to Tax Reform: The Concept of Tax Expenditure* (Cambridge, MA: Harvard University Press).

Tanzi, Vito, 1965, "Savings, Investment and Taxation in Underdeveloped Countries." *Kyklos*, 18:2, 205–226, republished in two other journals.

   1981, *Inflation and the Personal Income Tax: An International Perspective* (Cambridge: Cambridge University Press).

   1987, "The Response of Other Industrial Countries to the US Tax Reform Act." *National Tax Journal*, XL:3, 339–355.

   1995, *Taxation in an Integrating World* (Washington: The Brookings Institutions).

   2001, "Globalization, Technological Developments and the Work of Fiscal Termites." *Brooklyn Journal of International Law*, XXVI:4.

   2010, *Russian Bears and Somali Sharks: Transition and Other Passages* (New York: Jorge Pinto Books Inc.).

   2011, *Government Versus Markets: The Changing Economic Role of the State* (Cambridge: Cambridge University Press).

   2014a, "The Laffer Curve Muddle," in *A Handbook of Alternative Theories of Public Economics*, edited by Francesco Forte , Ram Mudambi, and Pietro Maria Navarra (Cheltenham: Edward Elgar).

   2014b, "Fiscal Policy for Entrepreneurship and Equitable Growth," in *Management and Economic Policy for Development*, edited by Grzegorz W. Kolodko (New York: Nova Publishers).

   2015, "Hayek and the Economic Role of the State: Some Comparisons with Keynes in Europe, Switzerland and the Future of Freedom," in *Essays in Honor of Tito Tettamanti* (Torino: IBL Libri).

   2018a, *Termite of the State: How Complexity Leads to Inequality* (Cambridge: Cambridge University Press).

   2018b, *The Ecology of Tax Systems* (Cheltenham, UK: Edward Elgar).

   2022, *Fragile Futures: The Uncertain Economics of Disasters, Pandemics and Climate Change* (New York: Cambridge University Press).

Tanzi, Vito and Ludger Schuknecht, 2000, *Public Spending in the 20th Century: A Global Perspective* (Cambridge: Cambridge University Press).

Taussig, F. W., 1892, *The Tariff History of the Unites States* (New York: G. P. Putnam and Sons).

Tobin, James and W. Allen Wallis, 1968, *Welfare Programs: An Economic Appraisal* (Washington, DC: The American Enterprise Institute).

Vance, J. D., 2016, *Hillbilly Elegy: A Memoir of a Family and Culture in Crisis* (New York: HarperCollins Publishers).

Veblen, Thorstein, 1899, *The Theory of the Leisure Class* (New York: Macmillan).

Vickrey, W. S., 1962, "One Economist View of Philanthropy," in *Philanthropy and Public Policy*, edited by F. G. Dickinson (New York: National Bureau of Economic Research), pp. 40–44.

Von Mises, Ludwig, 1988, *Two Essays by Ludwig von Mises* (Auborn, AL: Praxeology Press).

Weber, Max, [1923] no date, *General Economic History*, translated by Frank H. Knight (New York: Collier Books).

[1958] 2002, *Protestant Ethic and the Spirit of Capitalism* (New York: Penguin Press).

Weisbach, David and Jacob Nussim, 2004, "The Integration of Tax and Spending Programs." *The Yale Law Journal*, 113:5, 955–1028.

Weitz, Eric D., 2019, *A World Divided: The Global Struggle for Human Rights in the Age of Nation-States* (Princeton: Princeton University Press).

Winch, Donald, 1972, "Marginalism and the Boundaries of Economic Science." *History of Political Economy*, 4:2.

Woods, Thomas, Jr., ed., 2010, *Back on the Road to Serfdom: The Resurgence of Statism* (Wilmington, DE: ISI Books).

Woodward, Bob, 2000, *Maestro: Greenspan's Fed and the American Boom* (New York: Simon & Schuster).

Wunder, Haroldene, 2001, "Tanzi (1987): A Retrospective." *National Tax Journal*, 54:4, 763–770.

Yeh, Chen, Claudia Macaluso, and Brad Hershbein, 2022, "Monopsony in the US Labor Market." *The American Economic Review*, 112:7, 2099–2138.

Yu, Qiuping, Shawn Markad, and Masha Shunko, 2022, "Evidence on the United Labor Scheduling Implications of the Minimum Wage." *Cato Institute Research Briefs in Economic Policy*, June 1.

Index

Printed in the USA
CPSIA information can be obtained
at www.ICGtesting.com
LVHW090847081124
795688LV00077B/136